THE GREENHAVEN PRESS

Literary Companion

TO WORLD LITERATURE

READINGS ON

NIGHT

Wendy Mass, *Book Editor*

David L. Bender, *Publisher*

Bruno Leone, *Executive Editor*

Bonnie Szumski, *Series Editor*

Greenhaven Press, Inc., San Diego, CA

Every effort has been made to trace the owners of copy-
righted material. The articles in this volume may have
been edited for content, length, and/or reading level. The
titles have been changed to enhance the editorial purpose.
Those interested in locating the original source will find
the complete citation on the first page of each article.

Library of Congress Cataloging-in-Publication Data

Readings on Night / Wendy Mass, book editor.
      p.   cm. — (The Greenhaven Press literary
companion to world literature.)
      Includes bibliographical references and index.
      ISBN 0-7377-0369-5 (pbk. : acid-free paper). —
ISBN 0-7377-0370-9 (lib. : acid-free paper)
      1. Wiesel, Elie, 1928–   Un di òelò hoò geshòign.
2. Wiesel, Elie, 1928–   . 3. Holocaust, Jewish (1939–
1945)—Personal narratives—History and criticism.
I. Mass, Wendy, 1967–   . II. Series.
D804.196 .W547   2000
940.53'18'092—dc21
                                                        99-055870
                                                           CIP

Cover photo: Corbis/Matthew Mendelsohn

Copyright ©2000 by Greenhaven Press, Inc.
PO Box 289009
San Diego, CA 92198-9009
Printed in the U.S.A.

❝If we forget, we shall be forgotten. If we remember, then they will remember us.❞

—Elie Wiesel

CONTENTS

Chapter 5: The Legacy of *Night*

Foreword

*"'Tis the good reader that
makes the good book."*

Ralph Waldo Emerson

The story's bare facts are simple: The captain, an old and scarred seafarer, walks with a peg leg made of whale ivory. He relentlessly drives his crew to hunt the world's oceans for the great white whale that crippled him. After a long search, the ship encounters the whale and a fierce battle ensues. Finally the captain drives his harpoon into the whale, but the harpoon line catches the captain about the neck and drags him to his death.

A simple story, a straightforward plot—yet, since the 1851 publication of Herman Melville's *Moby-Dick*, readers and critics have found many meanings in the struggle between Captain Ahab and the whale. To some, the novel is a cautionary tale that depicts how Ahab's obsession with revenge leads to his insanity and death. Others believe that the whale represents the unknowable secrets of the universe and that Ahab is a tragic hero who dares to challenge fate by attempting to discover this knowledge. Perhaps Melville intended Ahab as a criticism of Americans' tendency to become involved in well-intentioned but irrational causes. Or did Melville model Ahab after himself, letting his fictional character express his anger at what he perceived as a cruel and distant god?

Although literary critics disagree over the meaning of *Moby-Dick*, readers do not need to choose one particular interpretation in order to gain an understanding of Melville's novel. Instead, by examining various analyses, they can gain

9

numerous insights into the issues that lie under the surface of the basic plot. Studying the writings of literary critics can also aid readers in making their own assessments of *Moby-Dick* and other literary works and in developing analytical thinking skills.

The Greenhaven Literary Companion Series was created with these goals in mind. Designed for young adults, this unique anthology series provides an engaging and comprehensive introduction to literary analysis and criticism. The essays included in the Literary Companion Series are chosen for their accessibility to a young adult audience and are expertly edited in consideration of both the reading and comprehension levels of this audience. In addition, each essay is introduced by a concise summation that presents the contributing writer's main themes and insights. Every anthology in the Literary Companion Series contains a varied selection of critical essays that cover a wide time span and express diverse views. Wherever possible, primary sources are represented through excerpts from authors' notebooks, letters, and journals and through contemporary criticism.

Each title in the Literary Companion Series pays careful consideration to the historical context of the particular author or literary work. In-depth biographies and detailed chronologies reveal important aspects of authors' lives and emphasize the historical events and social milieu that influenced their writings. To facilitate further research, every anthology includes primary and secondary source bibliographies of articles and/or books selected for their suitability for young adults. These engaging features make the Greenhaven Literary Companion Series ideal for introducing students to literary analysis in the classroom or as a library resource for young adults researching the world's great authors and literature.

Exceptional in its focus on young adults, the Greenhaven Literary Companion Series strives to present literary criticism in a compelling and accessible format. Every title in the series is intended to spark readers' interest in leading American and world authors, to help them broaden their understanding of literature, and to encourage them to formulate their own analyses of the literary works that they read. It is the editors' hope that young adult readers will find these anthologies to be true companions in their study of literature.

INTRODUCTION

When Elie Wiesel's *Night* was first published in English in 1960, it sold only a few hundred copies a year. Today, at the beginning of the twenty-first century, it sells hundreds of thousands of copies each year and stands alongside Anne Frank's *Diary of a Young Girl* as a crucial Holocaust memoir. From the moment Wiesel picked up his pen to write *Night*, he has devoted his life to making sure people do not forget the Holocaust and its lessons. Students continue to study the causes and effects of the Holocaust in their history books, but by bringing *Night* into the classroom and presenting teenagers with a protagonist their own age, teachers dedicated to bringing the message closer to home hope to introduce new generations to the reality of the concentration camps.

One reason for *Night*'s continued success is its accessibility. Written from the viewpoint of a fifteen-year-old boy, Eliezer, the language is straightforward and easy to follow. At a little over a hundred pages, it is quickly read. The book does not set out to present every one of Eliezer's emotions or experiences in the camps. Rather, it focuses on a few days, a few events, a few conversations. The reader must fill in the blanks from the scenes they are presented with. Wiesel explains that what is left unsaid is as important as what is said.

In the essays presented in this book, a wide range of Holocaust scholars and educators explore distinct aspects of *Night* and its author. Some literary critics view *Night* solely as an autobiography, and have therefore focused their commentaries on aspects of the story itself. Others consider the author's technique from the perspective of literary criticism. Still others focus on *Night*'s place in the canon of Holocaust literature. This Literary Companion also includes a plot summary and character breakdown, along with a chronology of relevant events in Wiesel's life and of the Holocaust in general. Taken together—along with Wiesel's own words— the reader will be able to approach the study of *Night* from many angles as well as gain a full understanding of the power of Wiesel's memoir and the ability of one man's words to instill memory.

ELIE WIESEL: A BIOGRAPHY

In the nearly forty years of Elie Wiesel's writing life, he has written nearly as many books. This poor, shy boy from the Carpathian Mountains, Transylvania, became an adviser to presidents and prime ministers and queens, and a voice of memory for the whole world. One of America's most prolific writers and well respected lecturers, he is best known in literary and religious circles as the author of *Night*, his powerful 1958 Holocaust memoir. In the political arena, he is a messenger of peace, speaking out against human rights abuses wherever they occur. In addition to numerous literary and peace prizes, Wiesel is the recipient of nearly eighty honorary doctorates from prestigious universities around the world.

A CHILD IS BORN

Elie Wiesel was born to Shlomo and Sarah Wiesel on September 30, 1928, in Sighet, Transylvania, what was then and is now northern Romania. At the time of World War II the small mountain village belonged to Hungary. Shlomo Wiesel was a much-loved shopkeeper in Sighet, and was often called on to advise the townspeople. Elie didn't spend as much time with his father as he would have liked, since Shlomo was a busy and religious man, always involved with affairs of the town or synagogue. It was his mother, Sarah, whom Wiesel considered his closest ally. He also had two older sisters, Hilda and Bea, and one younger sister, named Tzipora. About his younger sister, Wiesel says, "We all loved her madly. My father treated her with a special tenderness, always had time for her. . . . He pampered her, spoiled her, as did we. Perhaps we sensed that time was short, that we had to shower her with all the love and all the joys and favors of which she would soon be deprived."[1]

By the time Wiesel was three years old, he was learning to read Hebrew and soon became immersed in religious training. The community of Sighet had a large population of Hasidic Jews whose faith and religious practice were all-important. A shy, sickly child, Wiesel loved studying the Torah and the Talmud, and his favorite activity was listening to his grandfather's Hasidic stories and songs. He often felt himself an outsider among the other students, and would give them small gifts in the hope of being liked and included. When Wiesel was twelve years old, he decided he wanted to study cabala, the Jewish teachings. However, Jewish tradition proclaims the task should be taken only by men over forty. Cabala is extremely taxing theologically and a certain amount of maturity is needed to process it. But Wiesel found a teacher anyway. Together with two other boys Wiesel dove headfirst into the world of mysticism.

HITLER'S THREAT

Even after the outbreak of World War II and Adolf Hitler's war against the Jews, most of Sighet was ignorant of the severity of the threat it faced. Anti-Semitism (blind hatred of Jews) had always been part of their lives, so they were used to it on a minor level. They did not realize that Hitler had put in motion his plan to exterminate the Jews of Europe. Wiesel's father was aware that some Jews were in danger, and was briefly involved in smuggling Jews out of Poland. Even though he was sent to jail for a few months for his actions, he still believed his family would be safe in Sighet.

The Nazi menace reached Sighet for the first time in 1942, when all the foreign Jews were rounded up and taken away by train. The handyman of the synagogue, Moshe, was among the deportees; after a period of fear and outrage, however, life returned to normal for the remaining townspeople. Until, that is, a very changed Moshe returned. He explained that the Jews had been forced to dig their own mass grave and were then shot and thrown into it. He himself was shot in the leg, but pretended to be dead until the German soldiers left. He made his way back to Sighet to warn everyone. Unfortunately, no one, not even his friend Wiesel, believed Moshe's story. They just couldn't believe human beings could be that evil. They were soon to learn otherwise.

In 1944 the German army invaded Sighet and forced the Jews to move into ghettos, fenced-off sections of town. They were made to wear a yellow star on their clothes, which would mark them as Jews. Wiesel's father told the family not to worry, and for a while, even in the ghetto, life ran smoothly. Suddenly, however, the Jews were told to prepare for deportation. A Christian maid, whom the Wiesels considered part of their family, offered to hide them from the soldiers. Wiesel's father refused, believing as long as they stayed together they would be all right. Wiesel and his family were herded into overcrowded cattle cars on the last convoy out of town. The train left Hungary and headed into Poland, where it finally reached its destination: Birkenau, the extermination section of the largest Nazi concentration camp, Auschwitz. The first sight that greeted Wiesel was a truckload of live babies and children being emptied into a huge fire. The shock and the screams and the smell of burning flesh was worse than any nightmare he could conjure. Wiesel's mother, sisters, and beloved grandmother were sent off in one direction, while he clung to his father's hand and lined up with the men. This was the last time he would ever see his mother and younger sister, Tzipora. The fifteen-year-old vowed at that moment that he would never forget the horrors that he witnessed that night.

A PRISONER OF DEATH

Years later he still can't think of that night without rage and despair. "In their barbarous madness they cast living Jewish children into specially tended furnaces. I see them now and I curse the killers, their accomplices, the indifferent spectators who knew and kept silent, and Creation itself, Creation and those who perverted and distorted it. I feel like screaming, howling like a madman so that the world, the world of murderers, might know it will never be forgiven."[2] Wiesel claims that when he gets to heaven he will stand before God and say, "Look! Look at the flames that burn and burn, hear the mute cries of Your children as they turn to dust and ashes."[3]

Stripped of their clothes and dignity, the prisoners were tattooed with an identification number on their forearms. From that point on, Wiesel was known to the SS guards only as A-7713. He and his father, spared the gas chamber, were sent a few miles away to a slave labor camp called Buna, where they worked in a warehouse sorting electrical supplies. Wiesel was later transferred to a heavy labor unit. Wiesel tried not to think about what had happened to the rest of his family and was grateful for his father's presence, company he had never had before. "I could cope thanks to my father. I would see him coming with his heavy gait, seeking a smile, and I would give it to him. He was my support and my oxygen, as I was his."[4]

Wiesel was constantly hungry, since the inmates were fed only black coffee in the morning and a crust of bread with watery soup at night. Death by starvation was an hourly occurrence. Every few weeks a "selection" was held, a process directed by Joseph Mengele, a notoriously cruel SS medical officer who decided who would be sent to the gas chambers and who was still fit to work. Wiesel tried to lay low and not draw any attention to himself. Any perceived infraction of the rules meant torture or death. Many times he didn't escape the guards' wrath and was beaten or whipped. His father was not spared this treatment either. Wiesel tried to remain religious in the camp, mostly to please his father. But he couldn't help wondering why God had deserted them. Later he wrote, "In a strange way I never stopped believing in God, but I stopped believing in God as always merciful, charitable and generous and kind and good and just."[5]

In January 1945 Wiesel had required surgery on his leg. While recovering in the camp hospital, he learned that the Russian army was approaching and that the prisoners were being transferred to a camp in Germany. He was given the option of staying behind in the hospital, but Wiesel was certain that the SS guards would kill the sick patients rather than let the Russians find them. He and his father decided to leave with the others. Wiesel later learned that the patients left behind were not killed but liberated by the Russian army a few days later.

Wiesel and his father joined twenty thousand other prisoners on a death march. They ran for forty-two miles as snow and icy winds whipped around them. The pain from Wiesel's swollen leg was excruciating, but with his father's help he forced himself to keep running. Anyone who slowed down was shot or trampled. Finally the prisoners were herded onto cattle cars and shipped to Buchenwald, a concentration camp in central Germany. It was now Wiesel's turn to help his father, who had become very ill with dysentery. He appealed to the doctors to help him, tried to get him to eat, and protected him fiercely from the other prisoners. His dedication earned him a severe beating from a guard and in the end he couldn't save his father. "I was sixteen years old when my father died. My father was dead and the pain was gone. I no longer felt anything. Someone had died inside me, and that someone was me."[6]

A few months later, in April 1945, Buchenwald was liberated by the American army. The war was over and the prisoners in the concentration camps were freed. Wiesel doesn't remember feeling joy; he was too empty and too hungry. He wound up in a makeshift army hospital set up nearby. The army doctors treated him for blood poisoning and he wavered for weeks between life and death.

FREEDOM

Wiesel was well cared for in the hospital and was soon well enough to leave Germany with the rest of the rescued children. A long ride in a luxurious train car brought them to France. At the station stops strangers offered hot food to the traumatized and still weak children. The young displaced survivors were housed and fed and treated with love and respect. Wiesel asked for, and received, prayer books and other religious material. It took a while before he could eat a meal without hiding some of it for later. He returned to his studies and played games with his new friends. One day a journalist came by and took a picture of Wiesel playing chess. By an amazing coincidence, his sister Hilda saw the picture in the newspaper in Paris and tracked him down. Each had assumed the other was dead. He learned that his other sister, Bea, had survived as well, and had returned to Sighet to look for him. They were reunited a few months later.

With the help of a tutor, Wiesel learned French. To make some money, he began holding Bible study classes and led a choir. He studied religion under a mysterious and brilliant teacher named Shushani, whom he now credits with making him the person and the Jew that he is today. Many of his friends went to Palestine (soon to become the State of Israel), but he wasn't ready to leave France and what was left of his family. Instead, he enrolled at the Sorbonne and lived the life of a very poor (and often deeply depressed) college student. While still in school, he became a journalist and finally felt useful. On May 14, 1948, Israel declared itself an independent Jewish state, and Wiesel received the news with tears of joy. He soon boarded a ship for his first visit to Israel and decided to become a foreign correspondent for Israeli newspapers.

A WRITER IS BORN

As a foreign correspondent, Wiesel traveled around the world and met fascinating people. In 1954, he interviewed the Catholic writer François Mauriac, who had received the Nobel Prize in literature in 1952. Mauriac's conversation focused on the suffering of Jesus on the cross, and finally an outraged Wiesel responded angrily that no one talks about the million Jewish children who suffered 6 million times worse only ten years ago. He tried to leave the apartment building but Mauriac reached out to him and begged to hear his story. As Wiesel told the barest outline of his experiences, the old man wept. Mauriac told him he must tell his story. He must speak out. Wiesel argued that he had vowed not to write for ten years, which he felt would be "long enough to see clearly. Long enough to learn to listen to the voices crying inside my own. Long enough to regain possession of my memory. Long enough to unite the language of man with the silence of the dead."[7]

The ten years were nearly up by that time, and Wiesel took Mauriac's advice not to wait any longer. He finally consented to write about his experiences at the hands of the Nazis, and once he allowed himself to put down the words, they just kept coming. The resulting memoir, *And the World Remained Silent,* written in Yiddish, was nearly eight hundred pages long. Shortened by almost seven-eighths, it was published in French in 1958 and in English in 1960, under the name *Night.* Mauriac provided the foreword to the memoir, which prompted the literary community to take notice of the slim volume by an unknown writer. Though very short, with frequent gaps between sections, Wiesel believes that was the only way he could truly tell the story: "Writing is not like painting where you add. It is not what you put on the canvas that the reader sees. Writing is more like a sculpture where you remove, you eliminate in order to make the work visible. Even those pages you remove somehow remain."[8]

At first people shied away from *Night,* in part because the subject matter is so disturbing and people did not want postwar reminders of wartime horrors. But eventually the book began to alter the way people looked at the Holocaust, and it became a crucial historical document. Today it is a staple of high school literature and history classes. It continues to receive high praise from politicians, theologians, fellow writers, and Holocaust scholars. *Night* also had the effect of spurring other Holocaust survivors to write their own eye-witness accounts of Nazi brutality. Wiesel encourages every survivor he meets to tell their story, and in fact, he will pub-lish them himself. Influential talk show host and author Oprah Winfrey recently told Wiesel, "I read your book *Night*. I think I will never be the same again. I believe that every human being should read it, to somehow connect and expe-rience what the world stood by in indifference and allowed to happen."[9]

WELCOME TO AMERICA

While in New York to cover a story in 1956, Wiesel was hit by a taxicab and spent a year recuperating. He published his first novel, *Dawn*, in 1961; his second novel, 1962's *The Accident*, is about a Holocaust survivor who is hit by a car. These two novels and almost all the rest to come dealt on some level with the Holocaust. Though not clearly autobio-graphical like *Night*, they are informed by Wiesel's experi-ences and unique insights.

He became an American citizen in 1963 (almost by de-fault because his French visa had expired) and worked as a reporter for a newspaper in New York City. The following year Wiesel made his first trip back to his native Sighet, once again a part of Romania, and found that life went on as usual, and that nobody seemed to miss all those who had been killed. Strangers lived in his house, using his parents' old furniture. He wrote about his perceptions in his 1970 col-lection of essays, *One Generation After*. He also visited Rus-sia and was shocked at the anti-Semitism that flourished there. The resulting book, *The Jews of Silence*, forced the world to wake up to their plight.

In 1969 he married Marion E. Rose, also a concentration camp survivor. Marion translated his books—always written in French—into English. Very much a team, she still trans-lates his books today. In 1970 *A Beggar in Jerusalem* won Wiesel the prestigious French literary honor, the Prix Medicis. In 1972, Wiesel was thrilled to welcome their son Shlomo-Elisha (named after Wiesel's father) into the world.

A MAN OF PEACE

By the early 1970s, Wiesel was speaking out as well as writ-ing about the horrors of war and hate and the Holocaust. In 1972 he began his teaching career at the City University of

New York, where he taught Jewish studies until 1976. Many of his students were children of survivors. Wiesel explained that they needed him to teach them Holocaust literature because their "parents are silent, and the children need to learn their truth, and live their life, and live their death."[10] He was then named Andrew W. Mellon Professor in the Humanities at Boston University, where he still teaches classes and lectures on philosophy and literature, rather than the Holocaust. A highly sought after and dedicated teacher, he will fly halfway around the world rather than miss a class. His lectures are always standing room only, and he never repeats a speech.

In 1979, Wiesel added "crusader for peace and justice" to his writing and teaching careers. Various activist groups were gaining attention by claiming that the Holocaust never happened. Wiesel refused to debate them, admitting that "I don't know how you react to all this. I can only tell you what one survivor feels—he is not sad, he is outraged."[11] Partly to counteract the outrageous lies, President Jimmy Carter created the Commission on the Holocaust, soon renamed the Holocaust Memorial Council. Wiesel was given the daunting task of chairing the commission, an honor that brought with it months of hard work, travel, and soul-searching. One of Wiesel's main tasks was to develop a museum in Washington, D.C., that would commemorate those lost in the Holocaust while serving as a reminder to mankind never to let it happen again. Wiesel led the commission on a trip to Europe and Russia to research and witness official memorials to the Holocaust, suggesting in some cases that local governments should do more to fulfill that duty. They also honored the memory of Swedish diplomat Raoul Wallenberg, a "Righteous Gentile" who saved thirty thousand Hungarian Jews by providing them with false papers and routes to safety.

The commission also initiated a new tradition. Each year there would be a Day of Remembrance. In his speech on the first commemoration, April 24, 1979, Wiesel told President Carter that "Memory may perhaps be our only answer, our only hope to save the world from ultimate punishment, a nuclear holocaust."[12]

In 1980, Wiesel traveled to Southeast Asia in a humanitarian effort to help starving Cambodian refugees. He went, he stated, because nobody came to help him when he was starving. He could not let victims' voices go unanswered.

The following year Wiesel was the honorary chairman of the World Gathering of Jewish Holocaust Survivors in Jerusalem. Thousands of survivors and their families came to share their stories and remember those lost.

MAKING A DIFFERENCE

In 1985, Wiesel made headline news when he confronted President Ronald Reagan at the White House. Wiesel was present to accept one of America's highest honors, the Congressional Medal of Achievement. But when he learned that President Reagan was about to embark on a trip to Germany that would include a visit to a cemetery in Bitburg where many SS soldiers are buried, he couldn't keep quiet. As he graciously accepted his medal he implored the president not to go, saying that his place is with the victims of the SS. The president insisted that his plans were inflexible and the trip took place. He also visited the site of the concentration camp Bergen-Belsen, and stressed that people must never forget the evils that took place during the Holocaust. Through this incident, Wiesel's name became even more well known as the issue was widely discussed in the media.

Wiesel's efforts to stir the moral consciousness of the world through his books, lectures, and deeds was recognized in 1986 when he was awarded the Nobel Peace Prize. As he received the award in Oslo, Norway, he summed up his life's mission:

> Do I have the right to represent the multitudes who have perished? Do I have the right to accept this great honor on their behalf? I do not. That would be presumptuous. No one may speak for the dead, no one may interpret their mutilated dreams and visions. . . . The world [knew what was happening in the concentration camps] and remained silent. And that is why I swore never to be silent whenever and wherever human beings endure suffering and humiliation. We must always take sides. Neutrality helps the oppressor, never the victim. Silence encourages the tormentor, never the tormented.[15]

With the money accompanying the Nobel award, Wiesel and his wife Marion created the Wiesel Foundation for Humanity. The foundation sponsors conferences and meetings around the world on various humanitarian topics geared toward education and opposition to hate and oppression. The proceeds from almost all of Wiesel's lecturing and publishing endeavors go to charitable pursuits.

New York City was proud of its new Nobel Prize w

and Wiesel was invited to throw the first ball of the Mets vs. Red Sox World Series at Shea Stadium. At his son's urging, Wiesel agreed. He recalls being scared that he would embarrass himself. Instead, he did a great job, and his picture appeared in *Sports Illustrated* with the caption, "For a man of peace, he threw a nasty palmball."[14]

Wiesel's next high honor came in 1992, in the form of the Congressional Medal of Freedom, presented to him by President George Bush. That same year Wiesel traveled to Bosnia, in the former Yugoslavia, to see firsthand the "ethnic cleansing" perpetrated against Bosnian Muslims by militant Serbs. He urged the newly elected Bill Clinton to help put an end to the atrocities, which seemed to him very similar to the Nazis' extermination of the Jews.

In 1993 Wiesel spoke passionately at the opening ceremony of the U.S. Holocaust Memorial Museum, a structure he had helped develop. President Clinton presided over the opening and from then on often consulted with Wiesel on matters of international ethics, and the two flew together to the funeral of Israeli prime minister Yitzhak Rabin in 1995.

That same year Wiesel published the first volume of his memoirs, *All Rivers Run to the Sea.* Constantly in demand, he travels the world lecturing and speaking out against inhumanity. At a lecture at the University of Pennsylvania, he posed a challenge to his rapt audience: "I fear that at some point in the year 2000, good, decent people among the gentiles, the very people we now call our friends, will say, 'You must let us forget what happened to your people in the 20th century. Our children cannot grow up with this knowledge.' And what will your answer be?"[15]

NOTES

1. Elie Wiesel, *Memoirs: All Rivers Run to the Sea.* New York: Alfred A. Knopf, 1995, p. 15.

2. Elie Wiesel, *Memoirs: All Rivers Run to the Sea,* p. 18.

3. Elie Wiesel, *Memoirs: All Rivers Run to the Sea,* p. 89.

4. ̄ ̄ ̄ l, *Memoirs: All Rivers Run to the Sea,* p. 81.

Jonathan Mahler, "A Master of 'And Yet': Elie Wiesel, ˙adox," *Forward,* November 10, 1995.

Memoirs: All Rivers Run to the Sea, p. 94.

4 Jew Today. New York: Random House, 1978, p. 15.

ᴐton, ed., *Writers at Work.* New York: Penguin

9. Quoted in Jonathan Mahler, "A Master of 'And Yet': Elie Wiesel, a Prophet of Paradox," *Forward*, November 10, 1995.

10. Elie Wiesel, *A Jew Today*, p. 40.

11. Elie Wiesel, *A Jew Today*, p. 46.

12. Irving Abrahamson, ed., *Against Silence: The Voice and Vision of Elie Wiesel*. New York: Holocaust Library, 1985, vol. 1, p. 35.

13. Elie Wiesel, "Wiesel Nobel Peace Prize Speech" in Historical Documents of 1986, Washington D.C.: *Congressional Quarterly*, Inc., 1987, pp. 1077-78.

14. Quoted in Yosef I. Abromowitz, "Is Elie Wiesel Happy?" *Moment*, February 28, 1994.

15. Quoted in Robert Leiter, "Wiesel: Judaism is not about catastrophe," *Jewish Exponent*, October 23, 1993.

CHARACTERS AND PLOT

Eliezer: The main character of the story. A deeply pious teen-age boy who barely survives internment in Auschwitz. He vows never to forget the atrocities against humanity that he witnessed.

Shlomo: Eliezer's father. A well-liked and highly respected storekeeper. He tries to take care of Eliezer in the camps, but eventually it is Eliezer who must take care of him. He dies of dysentery and abuse at the hand of a guard in Buchenwald.

Eliezer's Mother: She tries to keep her family's life moving as smoothly as possible in the ghetto. Eliezer assumes she was killed as soon as the convoy reached Birkenau, at Auschwitz.

Hilda and Bea: Eliezer's older sisters who helped their mother around the house and their father at his store. Eliezer is unaware of their fate once they reach the concentration camp and are separated.

Tzipora: Eliezer's younger sister who bravely prepares for deportation from her home. Comforted by her mother, she is led presumably to her death at Birkenau.

Moshe the Beadle: A handyman at the synagogue. A friend of Eliezer's who teaches him the mystical cabala, he is taken away by the Gestapo early in the war and returns to warn the town about the atrocities he witnessed. No one believes his stories.

Maria: A former housekeeper for the Wiesel family. A non-Jew, she is distraught by Jewish deportations and begs the Wiesels to hide at her house.

Madame Schachter: A distraught and hysterical woman on the train out of Sighet who screams about a horrible fire.

Akiba Drumer: An inmate who tries to keep the other prisoners' spirits up in the camps by singing Hebrew songs at night. He fails to escape one of the last "selections" and is killed. He asks his fellow prisoners to say the Kaddish, the Jewish prayer for the dead, for him after he goes.

Franek: The foreman at the warehouse where Eliezer and his father work. He quickly loses his initial compassion and forces Eliezer to give him the gold crown from his mouth.

Idek: A violent soldier in charge of Eliezer's unit. He whips Eliezer and beats his father.

Juliek: A friend of Eliezer's, and one of the musicians at Buna. He smuggles his violin with him on the final march, and the night before his death plays a beautiful tune.

Rabbi Eliahou: A beloved Polish rabbi whose son abandons him.

Yossi and Tibi: Brothers whose parents were killed. They befriend Eliezer when they work at the warehouse together.

Joseph Mengele: A cruel SS medical officer who oversees the "selections" and decides who lives and who dies.

PLOT SUMMARY

Night begins in 1941, two years after the outbreak of World War II, in the small town of Sighet, Transylvania, which was part of Hungary at the time. The main character, twelve-year-old Eliezer, is a happy, religiously devout Jewish boy studying the Torah (the Old Testament of the Bible) and Talmud, a collection of rabbinical teachings and commentaries. He loves his parents and three sisters dearly, and is looking forward to a life of study and prayer. A dose of teenage rebellion leads him to study the mystical teachings of the cabala with a poor handyman named Moshe the Beadle. Moshe teaches Eliezer to see things from many angles as they pore over the pages of the Zohar, a great mystical book of the cabala, together.

The next year, in 1942, the nonnative Jews of Sighet are deported under orders of the Nazis. The townspeople are sad to see them go, but don't worry about their safety. Eliezer is especially sad that Moshe was taken. A few months later, however, Moshe reappears. He has returned to say that everyone else in the transport had been killed, and that he escaped only by pretending to be dead. He came back to warn the others, but unfortunately, nobody, not even Eliezer, believes what they conclude is an absurd tale. Though the townspeople have heard reports of the war, they are optimistic that it will end soon and that they will be safe.

In the spring of 1944, however, German soldiers arrive in

Sighet. The Jews are soon forced to leave their homes and are moved into fenced-off sections of town called ghettos. Eliezer's family is lucky—their house is within the walls of the ghetto so they don't have to abandon their home. One night a man knocks on their sealed windows to warn them to leave town, but they can't open the window in time to receive his warning. One morning the Jews are told to wait outside in the hot sun until it is their turn to be shipped out. For the first time, they are treated cruelly and beaten. A non-Jewish housekeeper offers to hide Eliezer's family, but his father refuses, condemning the family to its fate.

During the long and disturbing train ride, a woman, Madame Schachter, continuously screams that there is a terrible fire. The others can't make her stop. When the train finally arrives at Auschwitz, a huge concentration camp in Poland, the deportees are shocked to see that there really is a fire. Eliezer watches in horror as young children are thrown to their deaths into the flames. The men are separated from the women; it is the last time Eliezer will ever see his mother and younger sister. He clings to his father for strength. His trust in God suddenly wavers for the first time in his life. How could God allow babies to be dumped in a fire? He vows never to forget the horrors he has witnessed that night.

Eliezer and his father pass the first "selection" and are allowed to live. They are forced to give up their clothes and don prison outfits. Instead of being called by name, an identification number is tattooed on each prisoner's arm. For a few weeks things are quiet. The prisoners eat tiny morsels of bread and soup and try to believe that their other family members are safe. Eventually, Eliezer and his father are led on a four-hour march to another camp called Buna, where, after they pass a medical exam, they are assigned light manual labor in a warehouse. The dentist keeps trying to take the gold crown from Eliezer's mouth, but Eliezer manages to hold onto it, knowing he might need it later as a bargaining tool.

The prisoners, always hungry and exhausted, try to keep out of the guards' way. Each day thousands are incinerated in the ovens only a few miles away at Auschwitz. Sometimes for no reason a guard will attack a prisoner, and one day Eliezer is beaten very badly. Another time it is his father who is beaten, and Eliezer can only stand and watch, knowing that if he protests his father will only suffer more. Soon Eliezer is forced to give up his gold crown, which isn't nearly as painful as the twenty-five lashes he receives when he accidentally walks in on a sexual encounter between a guard and a woman.

One day the Allies bomb the camp, but only one man who is trying to sneak extra food when the guards are away from their post, is killed. The SS often hang prisoners for one reason or another, but one day it is a child who is chosen. The prisoners are forced to watch as the life slowly drains from the "sad-eyed angel." If the inmates have any faith left in God, many lose it that day.

The Jewish holidays come and go, and Eliezer still can't accept God's silence. He refuses to fast on Yom Kippur and instead feels a heavy void where his love of God used to be. He is assigned to heavy manual labor and fears for his father back at the warehouse. Fortunately, they both pass the notorious Dr. Mengele's next "selection" and are not killed. But when it is time for the "selected ones" to be herded up, Eliezer's father's number is called. He gives a devastated Eliezer his knife and spoon before he is taken away. Somehow, he manages to convince the SS that he is still useful and is returned to the camp.

In the middle of an unbearably cold winter, Eliezer's foot becomes infected. He is admitted to the camp hospital, where he is shocked to recall that he used to sleep in a real bed with real sheets. A kind Jewish doctor performs surgery on Eliezer's foot and he is told to stay in the hospital for two weeks. But Eliezer is never given the chance to recuperate. The Russian army is approaching the camp, and the Germans have decided to move everyone to another camp, farther into German territory. Eliezer is given the choice to stay in the hospital (where his father could have joined him) or join the others for transfer. Fear that the sick prisoners will be killed by the SS guards leads the two to choose to leave the camp with the others. Had they stayed, they would have been freed by the Russians two days later.

In the pitch dark and icy cold, the prisoners are led on a seemingly endless running march. Anyone who falls behind the quick pace is instantly shot or trampled. The pain in Eliezer's foot is unbearable and he considers just giving up. His father convinces him to keep moving. When the prisoners are finally allowed to rest, many crowd into an abandoned

factory shed where Eliezer and his father struggle to stay
awake since they believe that if they fall sleep they may never
wake up. At the end of the march, they are led into the town
of Gleiwitz, and herded into barracks. Everyone—the living
and the dead—are piled on top of each other. It is there that
Eliezer hears the last tunes from his friend Juliek's violin.

After three days with no food or water, the prisoners are
rounded up again in the snow. Eliezer saves his father from
"selection" one last time, and the emaciated prisoners are
shoved into roofless cattle wagons, a hundred to a wagon.
Despair is great, and not many survive the trip. When the
train arrives at the new concentration camp, Buchenwald, in
Germany, only twelve prisoners are left alive in Eliezer's
wagon. Once through the gates, Eliezer has to shout at his
father to convince him not to curl up in the snow, for he will
surely die there. The prisoners are finally brought to the
barracks to sleep.

The next morning Eliezer searches for his father and finally finds him burning with fever. He has dysentery and is
very weak. Eliezer gives him some soup and coffee and tries
in vain to get medical help. The other prisoners steal his father's bread and Eliezer is furious. The guard suggests that
Eliezer should take his father's portions, since he will die
soon anyway, but Eliezer refuses. One night his father's
screams of pain are cut off by a blow to his head by one of
the guards. The next morning, to Eliezer's horror, his father
is taken to the crematorium. The brief relief that Eliezer
feels brings self-hatred.

For nearly three months Eliezer thinks of nothing but eating and sleeping. He no longer thinks about his family or
anything else. The Germans are losing the war, and on April
5, 1945, they start evacuating the prisoners again, in an effort to stay one step ahead of the advancing Allied armies.
The SS soldiers intend to blow up the camp before the Allies
reach it. On April 10, a band of prisoners attack the SS and
the guards flee. That evening, the American army liberates
the twenty thousand prisoners that remain. Eliezer is among
them. As he is about to eat the food his rescuers offer, Eliezer
becomes seriously ill. When he is finally able to get out of
his hospital bed, he looks at himself in a mirror for the first
time since he left the ghetto in Sighet. A living corpse stares
back at him.

CHAPTER 1

Major Themes

Loss of Innocence

Irving Halperin

Irving Halperin, an English and creative writing professor at San Francisco State University, establishes that *Night* is the story of one boy's loss of innocence. Before the concentration camp Eliezer had a concrete view of the world. He believed that if the Jews didn't cause any trouble they would be safe; after all, God would protect them. He thought he was living in a modern age where people looked out for each other. By the end of the book, he learned he was wrong on all counts.

Eliezer as a boy in Sighet, a small town in Transylvania, absorbed the religious beliefs of his teacher, Moché the beadle, at a Hasidic synagogue. Moché prescribed that one should pray to God for "the strength to ask Him the right questions."

> "Man raises himself toward God by the questions he asks Him," he [Moché] was fond of repeating. "That is the true dialogue. Man questions God and God answers. But we don't understand His answers. We can't understand them. Because they come from the depths of the soul, and they stay there until death. You will find the true answers, Eliezer, only within yourself!" (*Night*, 16)

Later, as a result of his experiences during the Holocaust, Eliezer would cease expecting to get answers to his questions; indeed, he would come to say that question and answer are not necessarily interrelated. Then what should men do—stop asking such questions? Not at all. The protagonists in the later novels, in *The Town Beyond the Wall* and *The Gates of the Forest*, contend that men must continue to pose them. But not to God, who, in the eyes of the Wieselean narrator, remained silent during the Holocaust. Rather, these questions must come out of the depths of men and be addressed to other men. For to be human, to exercise one's humanity, is to go on posing such questions, even in the face of the Absurd, of Nothingness.

Excerpted from *Messengers from the Dead: Literature of the Holocaust,* by Irving Halperin. Copyright ©1970 by the Westminster Press. Reprinted by permission of Westminster John Knox Press.

JUST LAY LOW

But such recognition for the protagonist was in the distant future. Meanwhile, in the beginning of *Night*, the boy Eliezer did not question Moché's teachings. He believed that as long as Jews studied and were pious no evil could touch them. The Germans proved he was mistaken when they occupied Sighet in the spring of 1944. In consequence, the first of Moché's teachings . . . to Eliezer was the notion that a Jew should live lowly, be self-effacing and inconspicuous. Certainly Moché was an "invisible" man. The narrator says of him: "Nobody ever felt embarrassed by him. Nobody ever felt encumbered by his presence. He was a past master in the art of making himself insignificant, of seeming invisible."

And yet remaining "invisible" did not help Moché; the Germans systematically disposed of him along with Sighet's entire Jewish population. In the beginning of the Occupation, Jews were ordered to wear yellow stars, then they were driven out of their homes and herded into ghettos. A "Jewish council" and Jewish police were imposed on them. Some of the populace desperately attempted to escape annihilation by stationing themselves in such places and at such tasks that would keep them out of sight. And they further deluded themselves by thinking: The Germans—after all, this was the twentieth century—would oppress them up to a certain point and no further. So the popular advice was: Just do what they tell you; they only kill those who put up resistance. But in the end, packs on their backs, the Jewish community was marched off to a transport center, jammed into cattle wagons, and sent off to concentration camps. Meekness, staying "invisible," had not worked. And it is as though Wiesel laments that here was another instance wherein the Jew contributed to his agelong fate as victim and "specialist" in suffering. Ought not the time come when the Jew will make history itself tremble—when, if need be, *he* will be the executioner? In sum, Eliezer learned from having undergone the Occupation and deportation, that it is useless to employ the disguises of the "invisible" Jew. And this recognition constituted the first major puncture of his heretofore innocent faith in the teachings of Moché.

DIDN'T GOD CARE?

[Fifteen-year-old Eliezer believed in God] before he came to Auschwitz. But there, in hell on earth, that faith was consumed in the flames that consumed children. There "God" was the official on the train ramp who separated life from death with a flick of a finger to the right or left. Yet some Jews continued to urge children to pray to God. "You must never lose faith," they said to Eliezer, "even when the sword hangs over your head. That's the teaching of our sages."

But could the sages have imagined the limitless depravity of the Nazis? Could they, in all their wisdom, have counseled a boy of fifteen on how to react to the mass burning of children? To see a child's head, arms, and legs go up in flame— that is an indisputable fact, a measurable phenomenon.

Did He care that children were being consumed by fire? This is the question raised by the narrator of *Night.* And if He does nothing to prevent the mass murder of children, Eliezer cries out: "Why should I bless His name?" This outcry is the sign of, as François Mauriac says in his foreword to the book, "the death of God in the soul of a child who suddenly discovers absolute evil." And this breakdown of religious faith calls forth Eliezer's resolve "never to forget."

> Never shall I forget that night, the first night in camp, which has turned my life into one long night, seven times cursed and seven times sealed. Never shall I forget that smoke. Never shall I forget the little faces of the children, whose bodies I saw turned into wreaths of smoke beneath a silent blue sky.
>
> Never shall I forget those flames which consumed my faith forever.
>
> Never shall I forget that nocturnal silence which deprived me, for all eternity, of the desire to live. Never shall I forget those moments which murdered my God and my soul and turned my dreams to dust. Never shall I forget these things, even if I am condemned to live as long as God Himself. Never.

So, too, on the eve of Rosh Hashanah, Eliezer, who until then had always been devoted to this holiday, thinks, bitterly:

> Why, but why should I bless him? In every fiber I rebelled. Because He has had thousands of children burned in His pits? Because He kept six crematories working night and day, on Sundays and feast days? Because in His great might He had created Auschwitz, Birkenau, Buna, and so many factories of death? How could I say to Him: "Blessed art Thou, Eternal, Master of the Universe, who chose us from among the races to be tortured day and night, to see our fathers, our mothers, our brothers, end in the crematory? Praised be Thy Holy Name, Thou Who hast chosen us to be butchered on Thine Altar?"

After Auschwitz, Eliezer could no longer speak of God's goodness or His ultimate purposes.

What is the immediate consequence of this loss of faith? Eliezer feels as though he were a lost soul condemned to wander in a haunted realm of darkness. Here the word "darkness" needs to be underscored, for it is a world at the poles from the one of "light" which Eliezer, as a student of the Cabbala and Talmud, inhabited in Sighet. By day the Talmud, and at night, by candlelight, he and his teacher Moché would study together, searching for "the revelation and mysteries of the cabbala." There was not only candlelight when they studied; the Talmud, the Zohar, the cabbalistic books themselves *were* light; they illuminated the nature of the "question" and suggested the answer; they seemed to draw Moché and Eliezer toward the shining realm of the eternal "where question and answer would become one."

But the light in *Night* is of brief duration; the atmosphere of the book is almost entirely that of blackness. The fires of Auschwitz consume the light, the religious faith, of Eliezer and leave him a "damned soul" wandering through a darkness where question and answer would *never* become one.

EVERY MAN FOR HIMSELF

What other kinds of disillusionment are experienced by Eliezer? I have already pointed out two—his realization that to be an "invisible" Jew did not protect one from the Nazis and, second, his turning away from God on witnessing the mass burning of children at Auschwitz. There was also his loss of faith in both the myth of twentieth-century civilized man and the tradition of the inviolable bonds between Jewish parents and children. Before coming to Auschwitz, Eliezer had believed that twentieth-century man was civilized. He had supposed that people would try to help one another in difficult times; certainly his father and teachers had taught him that every Jew is responsible for all other Jews. Until the gates of a concentration camp closed upon him he had no reason to doubt that the love between parents and children was characterized by sacrifice, selflessness, and utmost fealty.

But Auschwitz changed all that. There he was forced to look on while a young boy was tortured and then hanged—his death taking more than a half hour of "slow agony." There dozens of men fought and trampled one another for an extra ration of food. In one instance, he saw a son actually killing his elderly father over a portion of bread while other prisoners looked on indifferently. In Auschwitz the conduct of most prisoners was rarely selfless. Almost every man was out to save his own skin; and to do so he would steal, betray, buy life with the lives of others.

Eliezer's progressive disillusionment did not come about simply because of what he witnessed in Auschwitz; he did not only observe the breakdown of faith; he himself in part caused it to happen. Consider Eliezer's thoughts and conduct with respect to his father when both were concentration camp prisoners. Eliezer feels that his father is an encumbrance, an albatross, who jeopardizes his own chances for survival. The son himself is ailing, emaciated, and in attempting to look after the older man strains his own limited physical resources. Moreover, such efforts make him dangerously conspicuous—always a perilous condition for concentration camp prisoners. And yet he despises himself for not having lifted a hand when his elderly father was struck by a Kapo. He had looked on, thinking: "Yesterday I should have sunk my nails into the criminal's flesh. Have I changed so much, then?"

Eliezer's conflict of wanting to protect his father and, conversely, to be separated from him, is so desperate that when the father is on the verge of dying, the son feels ashamed to think: "If only I could get rid of this dead weight, so that I could use all my strength to struggle for my own survival, and only worry about myself." Again, when the dying man is struck with a truncheon by an officer, Eliezer, fearing to be beaten, stands still, like one paralyzed. Finally, when his father is taken off to the crematoria, the son cannot weep. Grief there is in him and yet he feels free of his burden. Thus another illusion is discarded by a boy who had been reared in a tradition that stresses loyalty and devotion to one's parents.

REVENGE OR RELEASE?

The death of his father leaves Eliezer in a state of numbness; he feels that nothing more can affect him. But there remains still another illusion he is to shed—the belief that on being liberated the prisoners would be capable of avenging themselves on the enemy. They had endured so much in order to live to the day of liberation. How often had the prisoners spoken to one another about what they would do to the Germans. And yet when Buchenwald is liberated, Eliezer observes with anger and disgust that his fellow prisoners are concerned only with bread and not revenge.

He has lost not only his father but also faith in God and humanity. Many of his previously untested beliefs in the staying powers of the "invisible" Jew, the unquestionable justice of God, the built-in restraints of twentieth-century civilization, and the enduring strength of familial bonds between Jewish parents and children have been peeled away. He will have to journey for a long time and through many lands before arriving at that point of retrospective clarity when he can even first frame the "right questions" concerning his season in hell. He will need to stand before some "false" gates before he can turn away from them. And yet, all through this time, he is to hold fast to the belief that his teacher Moché instilled in him: that there is an "orchard of truth," and that for entering the gate to this place every human being has his own key.

The Theme of Night

Ellen S. Fine

Ellen S. Fine is a French professor at The City University of New York and worked with Wiesel on the U.S. Holocaust Memorial Council. Fine contends that the title of Wiesel's book reflects the theme that the character experiences—a never-ending descent into the darkest of night. She demonstrates that Wiesel uses the motif of night as a metaphor for the horrors of the concentration camp and for the inner darkness that he must confront.

The theme of night pervades Elie Wiesel's memoir as suggested by the title itself, which encompasses the overall Holocaust landscape—[the concentration camp universe]—a world synonymous with methodical brutality and radical evil. The dark country presented to us is self-contained and self-structured, governed by its own criminal gods who have created laws based upon a death-dominated ideology. Wiesel uses the word night throughout his writing to denote this strange sphere, unreal and unimaginable in its otherworldliness. Wiesel notes, in *Harry James Cargas in Conversation with Elie Wiesel*, "Whenever I say 'night' I mean the Holocaust, that period. 'Night' has become a symbol of the Holocaust for obvious reasons. As we have said, a night has descended upon mankind, not only in Europe, but everywhere. Whoever was alive in those days has absorbed parts or fragments of that night. Night enveloped human destiny. Night is a symbol of that period, a frightening symbol. Whenever I try to speak of those nights, I simply say 'night.'" He speaks of that "kingdom of the night where one breathed only hate, contempt and self-disgust" in "A Plea for the Dead"; and in one of his speeches, refers to "the dark kingdom which . . . represented the other side of Sinai, the dark face of Sinai." "We were the children of night," he proclaims, "and we knew more about truth and the paths leading to it

Excerpted from *Legacy of Night*, by Ellen S. Fine. Copyright ©1982 by the State University of New York. Reprinted with permission from the author and SUNY Press.

than the wisest philosophers on earth."

Eliezer, the narrator of the book, is, in effect, a child of the night, who relates the journey from the friendly Jewish community tucked away in the mountains of Transylvania to Auschwitz—the frightening and foreign capital of the kingdom of night. During the course of the trip certain events take place which stand out in the narrator's memory and often occur during the nocturnal hours. The theme of night is linked to the passage of time in the account itself. Within the larger framework, more specific phases, characterized by the motifs of the *first* and *last* night, structure the descent into terror and madness, and point to the demarcations between the known and unknown.

Once Eliezer enters Auschwitz, he loses his sense of time and reality. Darkness envelops him and penetrates within: his spirit is shrouded, his God eclipsed, the blackness eternal. Pushed to his limits, the narrator experiences the *other* haunted and interminable night defined by French philosopher Maurice Blanchot as "the death that one does not find"; "the borders of which must not be crossed." The intermingling of particular nights with *Night*, the measuring of time alongside timelessness, corresponds to a style that interweaves a direct narration of events with subtle reflections upon the experience.

NIGHT'S SHADOWS ARE CAST

In 1941, when the narrative begins, Eliezer is a deeply Orthodox boy of twelve, living in the town of Sighet, situated on the Hungarian-Rumanian border. The word *night* is first mentioned with regard to his evening visits to the synagogue: "During the day I studied the Talmud, and at night I ran to the synagogue to weep over the destruction of the Temple" (*Night*, 14). While this nocturnal lamentation is part of a religious tradition, its prominent position in the text can be interpreted as a prediction of the bleak shadow cast upon Jewish communities throughout twentieth-century Europe.

Eliezer spends many of his evenings in the semidarkness of the synagogue where half-burned candles flicker as he converses with Moché, his chosen master of the Kabbala; they exchange ideas about the nature of God, man, mysticism, and faith. Night, here, exudes a poetic and pious atmosphere as the time for prayer, interrogation and dialogue within the context of the secure and the traditional. Indeed, the narrator's experience of benevolent night begins to change with Moché's expulsion from Sighet. Deported because he is a foreign Jew, Moché is sent to Poland, driven to a forest along with hundreds of other Jews, and shot in front of freshly dug pits. Wounded in the leg only, he rises from the mass grave and miraculously makes his way back to Sighet to recount what he calls "the story of my own death." "Jews, listen to me," he cries out. "It's all I ask of you, I don't want money or pity. Only listen to me" (17). No one in the *shtetl*, including Eliezer, believes his tale, and Moché is forced into silence, Wiesel's first example of the unheeded witness whose futile warnings predict the fate of the entire Jewish community. This occurs towards the end of 1942.

Without being explicit, Wiesel's narrative closely follows the historical events that led to the expulsion of the Hungarian Jews. The years 1942 and 1943 as rapidly described in the text were fairly normal for the Jews of Sighet. While anti-Jewish legislation was enacted and periods of calm alternated with those of turbulence, day still predominated over night. From 1938 to 1944, Hungarian prime ministers ranged from eager collaborators to those who collaborated reluctantly, resulting in cycles of despair and hope for the Jews who were unable to assess their situation realistically. In 1944 the Jewish community of Hungary was the only large group still intact. The circumstances changed drastically, however, in March, with the German takeover of the country and the installation of the pro-German Sztojay government, Adolph Eichmann, commander of the Special Action Unit *(Sondereinsatzkommando),* came to Hungary to personally carry out one of the most concentrated and systematic destruction operations in Europe. In the spring of 1944, with the end of the war in sight, the Nazis deported and eventually wiped out 450,000 Jews, 70 percent of the Jews of Greater Hungary. The Jews from the Carpathian region and Transylvania were among the first to be ghettoized and then rounded up. Of the fifteen thousand Jews in Sighet's community alone, about fifty families survived.

The Germans were notorious for their methods of deceiving their victims by dispelling notions of fear and creating the illusion of normality as they went about setting the machinery of extermination in motion. Eliezer speaks of life's returning to normal, even after the Nazis forced the Jews of Sighet into two ghettos fenced off from the rest of the population by barbed wire. At least, he remarks, Jews were living among their brothers and the atmosphere was somewhat peaceful. This deceptively secure setting was soon to be shattered.

FIRST AND LAST NIGHTS

"Night fell," says the narrator, describing an evening gathering of friends in the courtyard of his family's house in the large ghetto. A group of about twenty was listening attentively to tales told by his father, when suddenly a Jewish policeman entered and interrupted his father's story, summoning him to an emergency session of the Jewish council. "The good story he had been in the middle of telling us was to remain unfinished," Eliezer notes (22). . . .

Suspended in the midst of its natural flow, the father's story is a metaphor for Jewish life and lives abruptly brought to a standstill in the middle of the night. When the father returns at midnight from the council meeting, he announces news of the deportation to be held the following day.

From this point on, time is defined by the first and last night. Eliezer refers to "our last night at home," spent in the large ghetto after watching the first transport of victims parade through the streets under the blazing sun, the infernal counterpart to night. Then, there is the last evening in the small ghetto, where Eliezer, his parents, and three sisters observe the traditional Sabbath meal: "We were, we felt, gathered for the last time round the family table. I spent the night turning over thoughts and memories in my mind, unable to find sleep" (31).

Expelled from the small ghetto, Eliezer and his family, along with other members of the community, are thrown into cattle cars where they endure three long nights. Day is left far behind. The theme of night corresponds here to the reduction of space. Whereas the gentle gloom of the synagogue provided the framework for a boundless exploration of sacred doctrines, the ghetto period—in its progression from larger to smaller—serves as a transitional space, leading to the nailed-up doors of the cattle wagons, which plunge the prisoners into the confinement and extreme darkness of a night without limits.

The night of the cattle wagons is hallucinatory. Madame Schächter, a woman of fifty, who along with her ten-year-old son had been deported separately from her husband and two elder sons, starts to go mad. On the third and last night in the train, she screams out as if possessed by an evil spirit, conjuring up vivid images of fire and a furnace. Some of the men peer through the barred train window to see what Madame Schacter is pointing to, but all they can glimpse is blackness. Night is both within and without, surrounding the mad prophet who continuously cries out, as if to predict the end of the world, but who is forcefully silenced by those around her who do not want to believe in the foreboding signs. At the terminus, Birkenau–Auschwitz, Madame Schacter gives one last howl: "Jews, look! Look through the window! Flames! Look!" (36). As the train stops, the victims, in disbelief, observe red flames gushing out of the chimney into the black sky. . . .

A NEVER-ENDING NIGHT

When Eliezer sees the vivid flames leaping out of a ditch where little children are being burned alive, he pinches his face in order to know if he is awake or dreaming in this nightmarish atmosphere of "Hell *made immanent."* The young boy watches babies thrown into the smouldering pits and people all around murmuring *Kaddish* (the Jewish prayer for the dead) for themselves—the living dead—as they slowly move in a kind of *danse macabre.* They give the eerie impression that they are participating in their own funeral. For a moment, the narrator contemplates throwing himself on the barbed wire, but the instinct for survival prevails. As he enters the Holocaust kingdom on that first night he recites a ritualistic incantation, which marks his initiation into one long and never-ending night and commits him to remember it always:

> Never shall I forget that night, the first night in camp, which has turned my life into one long night, seven times cursed and seven times sealed. Never shall I forget that smoke. Never shall I forget the little faces of the children, whose bodies I saw turned into wreaths of smoke beneath a silent blue sky.
>
> Never shall I forget those flames which consumed my faith forever.
>
> Never shall I forget that nocturnal silence which deprived me, for all eternity, to the desire to live. Never shall I forget those moments which murdered my God and my soul and turned my dreams to dust. Never shall I forget these things, even if I am condemned to live as long as God Himself. Never.

This invocation summarizes the principal themes of Wiesel's first book, joining the theme of night to those of fire, silence, and the death of children, of God, and of the self. The moment of arrival designates the end of the reality-oriented structure of "outer" night, and the shift to "inner" night, in which time is suspended. As dawn breaks Eliezer observes: "So much had happened within such a few hours that I had lost all sense of time. When had we left our houses? And the ghetto? And the train? Was it only a week? One night—*one single night?* . . . Surely it was a dream" (46).

Indeed, like a dream sequence, the events of the camp journey have been accelerated and condensed into a short interval. "One of the most astonishing things," says Wiesel, "was that we lost all sense not only of time in the French meaning of the word, of *durée*, but even in the concept of years. . . . The ten-year-old boy and the sixty-year-old man not only looked alike, felt alike and lived alike, but walked alike. There was a certain 'levelling.'" This levelling process seems to occur in one night, a notion often repeated by the author:

> In a single night, a single hour, one acquires knowledge and grows up. The child finds himself an old man. From one day to the next, familiar structures and concepts vanish, only to reappear in different forms. One gets used to the new order in spite of everything.

The concept of time that governs life in normal conditions thus changes radically in the concentrationary universe. But even more important than time is the highly organized and methodological procedure that deprives an individual of his humanness and transforms him into a thing while still alive. The *défaite du moi*, the "dissolution of the self," is the worst kind of living death and is a recurring theme in Holocaust literature.

After one single night in Auschwitz, Eliezer is turned into a subhuman, identified only by an anonymous number. . . . His spirit is arrested in the confines of night: the empire of darkness has taken possession of his inner being. For the boy of fifteen, history has stopped.

THE VERY LAST NIGHT

Although time is essentially abolished in the kingdom of death, the narrator nevertheless continues to structure outer reality in the account itself by noting the nights that mark the principal stages of the trip. After three weeks in Auschwitz, he and his father are sent in a work transport to Buna, where they spend several weeks. The Germans finally evacuate the camp as Russian troops approach. Before the long cold voyage to Buchenwald, Eliezer meditates on the motif of *the last night:*

> The last night in Buna. Yet another last night. The last night at home, the last night in the ghetto, the last night in the train, and, now, the last night in Buna. How much longer were our lives to be dragged out from one 'last night' to another? [89]

The march from Buna to Buchenwald takes place in blackness, amid glacial winds and falling snow. The boy realizes that the night he is leaving will be replaced by one even more unfathomable on the other side; the *invisible darkness* of the tomb. As the procession winds its way through the thick snow, numerous corpses are strewn upon its trail. After several days without food or water, the remaining prisoners are thrown into open cattle cars and transported to Buchenwald. For the starved skeletons who speed through the frozen landscape, "days were like nights and the nights left the dregs of their darkness in our souls" (105). Suddenly, on the last day of this seemingly endless journey, a fierce cry rises up from among the inert bodies of the entire convoy—a collective death rattle that seems to emanate from beyond the grave. This shared song of death when no hope is left is a protest to the world which has abandoned them. A brutal expression of the agony of those who have reached their limits, this massive convulsion *is* the primeval language of night. Finally, late in the evening, twelve survivors out of the hundred who started out reach Buchenwald.

The last night—and the most significant—is January 28, 1945. Eliezer's father, sick with dysentery, his head bloody from the blows of an SS guard, lies curled up miserably on his bunk bed. When his son awakens the next day, he realizes that his father has been carted away before dawn—perhaps still alive. It is the finality of this moment that virtually ends the narrative, plunging Eliezer into a realm where no light penetrates and where, on some level, the *child of night* remains for the rest of his life.

Initiation and Journey Motifs

Ted L. Estess

In order to best relay the story of Eliezer's experiences during the Holocaust, Ted L. Estess, author of the book *Elie Wiesel* and professor of religion and literature at the University of Houston, contends that Wiesel sets the story within the framework of two common themes—the Initiation and the Journey. Since the topic is so horrendous, Wiesel must find ways to tell it so that the horror is truly felt by the reader. By using these straightforward and established storytelling motifs, the reader better understands the main character's experiences.

Night tells what Eliezer underwent from the end of 1941 to April, 1945. To give form to the events Wiesel employs two familiar framing devices: those of a story or initiation and a story of journey. Inside these loose frames, Wiesel arranges the vignettes so that the story reads like a simple chronicle of Eliezer's experience. In order not to violate the experience he is relating, Wiesel refrains from imposing too severe an order on what was essentially an eruption of disorder in his world.

As an initiation story, the narrative explores the way in which a boy in his early teens goes through difficult trials to discover something new about himself, his people, and the world in which he is to live. Early in the story, the narrator suggests the importance of "initiation." The initiation to which he refers is conducted by Moché, Eliezer's teacher in the mysteries of the Kabbala and other secret matters of Jewish thought. Given the multitude of possible starting points for the story, it is crucial that Wiesel chose to open with Moché. The opening suggests that Wiesel wants us to read the story in the light of this picture of Eliezer as a religious seeker. What happens subsequently largely takes its mean-

Excerpted from *Elie Wiesel*, by Ted L. Estess. Copyright ©1980 by The Frederick Ungar Publishing Co. Reprinted by permission of Continuum International.

ing from the contrast between the experience of the Holocaust and Eliezer's early religious intensity.

This opening accentuates the initiation motif as well. The initiation to which the narrator refers involves a religious master and an earnest seeker. The master presumably knows something that the disciple does not; he is in touch with a hidden truth that can be discerned only after a long quest. Moché introduces Eliezer to the *Zohar*, the Book of Splendor, a mystical commentary on the first books of the Bible. As a Kabbalist, Moché is concerned with directing his student's soul toward the long, arduous ascent of the ladder of mystical enlightenment to a final disclosure of and union with the Eternal God. With the war, everything changes for the boy, but the change occurs downward toward darkness and nothingness. His initiation ends in despair and chaos, not hope and order; in isolation and horror, not in a community sustained by joy.

Under the tutelage of Moché, Eliezer had set out on a path leading to life. Instead, he enters into death, which takes over his existence. Death is everywhere in the camps: in the chimneys and fences, in the faces of the executioners, and in the eyes of the prisoners. Death floats in the clouds as the smoke from the chimneys slowly rises day after day. "Around me," Eliezer says, "everything was dancing a dance of death. It made my head reel. I was walking in a cemetery, among stiffened corpses, logs of wood." Silently but perceptibly, death enters the soul of Eliezer, and although he escapes physical death, he comes to belong more to the dead than to the living. At the end of the narrative, Eliezer looks at himself: "From the depths of the mirror, a corpse gazed back at me. The look in his eyes, as they stared into mine, has never left me."

THE LONG JOURNEY

The motif of initiation in *Night* is closely associated with the motif of journey. Before the Holocaust, Eliezer had set out on a spiritual journey whose destination was union with God. He had hoped that Moché would draw him "into eternity," away from the vicissitudes of bodily existence in time. Again, Eliezer's expectations are radically reversed, for he is forced into the worst of physical journeys. It begins with the ride in the cattle train to Auschwitz. After three weeks there, he walks to Buna, where he remains until January, 1945. During that time, the prisoners are marched to work outside the camp every day. In January, 1945, there is a savage march in the snow to Gleiwitz, followed closely by a ten-day ride in an open cattle car to Buchenwald. All the while, the young boy increasingly becomes obsessed with physical survival. Instead of a disclosure of divine mystery at the end of this journey, there is the death of God and a revelation of absolute evil at the heart of things. Instead of being transported out of the body and into the bliss of eternity, Eliezer moves steadily into degradation in an agonized physical world. . . .

THE STUDY OF KABBALAH

Eliezer's father didn't want him to study Kabbalah (also spelled Kabbala or Cabala or cabbala) until he was older.
In The Essential Kabbalah: The Heart of Jewish Mysticism, *professor Daniel C. Matt explains why.*

Traditionally, restrictions have been placed on the study of Kabbalah. Some kabbalists insisted that anyone seeking entrance to the orchard must be at least forty years old, though [the great 16th century kabbalist] Moses Cordovero stipulated twenty years. Other requirements included high moral standards, prior rabbinic learning, being married, and mental and emotional stability. The point is not to keep people away from Kabbalah, but to protect them. Mystical teachings are enticing, powerful, and potentially dangerous. The spiritual seeker soon discovers that he or she is not exploring something "up there," but rather the beyond that lies within. Letting go of traditional notions of God and self can be both liberating and terrifying. In the words of Isaac of Akko, "Strive to see supernal light, for I have brought you into a vast ocean. Be careful! Strive to see, yet escape drowning."

Daniel C. Matt, *The Essential Kabbalah: The Heart of Jewish Mysticism.* New Jersey: Castle Books, 1997, p. 17.

The change in his journey from a spiritual odyssey to a physical one is accompanied by a shift in Eliezer's stance on religious matters. At the beginning of the story, Eliezer takes the mysteries of the Kabbala to be the key to what is ultimately real. Later he speaks of "cabbalistic dreams." Earlier the holy days were the grandest days; later he views Yom Kippur as a "mirage." Eliezer radically questions religious beliefs, in part because he fears that the beliefs themselves contribute to the prisoners' destruction. Some victims submit willingly to the executioner because they see submission almost as a religious obligation.

But Eliezer's journey has spiritual dimensions as well. His spirit moves downward in an ever narrowing spiral. The first and last words of the English version of the book reflect one dimension of the contracting movement of the whole. The English version opens with the word "they" and ends with the word "me." "They" refers to the Jewish community in which Eliezer had lived. That community and the town of which it was a part linked him to the cosmos and to all of history. Its rituals and holy days imbued the passing of time with order and majesty. The world of that community was rich in stories, memories, and hopes for time and eternity.

Eliezer's movement into the night represents a gradual and seemingly inevitable contraction of this earlier world as one after another of its elements are stripped away. First the larger world of the town contracts into a ghetto, and then, it is left behind. Along the way, the religious community is destroyed, God absents Himself, the family is shattered. With the death of Eliezer's father, the spiraling down into the narrowing chasm is complete, and Eliezer is left "terribly alone in a world without God and without man." The journey is at its end.

The Theme of Silence

Simon P. Sibelman

Simon P. Sibelman, author of *Silence in the Novels of Elie Wiesel* begins his exploration on this theme with *Night*. He outlines how Wiesel first developed the notion of the Holocaust as a journey into ever deeper layers of silence. In *Night*, the prisoners quickly learn that any behavior other than silence will lead to their deaths. The silence of God, the inactivity of the world around them, and the stifling of their loved one's voices lead to a complete loss of self. Sibelman shows how Wiesel accomplishes this by weaving the sparse page layouts and the quick pacing of the sentences with the arc of the main character's tragic story.

Night is a testimony, a true story that mercilessly projects the reader into Hitler's inferno. Eugene Heimler suggests that "you can only create from something which is negative," and it does seem that Wiesel has used the evil of the Holocaust as the generative material for a work that recounts the deportation and destruction of a single Hungarian Jewish community and details the loss of the witness's identity, who is reduced to a physical and spiritual cadaver at the novel's end. As shall be demonstrated, this text is written in ever more negative layers of silence.

In *Night*, silence combines with sparse, tautly concise prose in which the naked horrors of the concentration camp infrequently appear, and from which hysteria and disingenuous sentimentality are banished. If the Holocaust as macro- /micro-experience reflecting on the human condition cannot be properly expressed, then one must shroud in silence those unspeakable elements. Wiesel has stated that uttering the ineffable is almost impossible. His idea elicits a paradox common to Holocaust literature. The survivor must bear witness to what has been; yet aspects of that reality cannot be told. Despite this, the author/survivor must strive to achieve what he or she can. Wiesel's acceptance of the need to speak, in spite of the imposed silence of Auschwitz and of the impotence of words to describe the event, highlights his personal quest for a sense of truth.

In *Night*, one is faced with silence in its most negative forms. It exists firmly as the novel's core. In referring to silence, I am not alluding to the high frequency of the word silence itself, but to those other structural features . . . described and employed by Wiesel to evoke silence, notably the white spaces and long pauses. Within the space of this slim volume, Wiesel interrupts the text with such blank spaces eighty-two times. Elsewhere, the author himself emphasizes the importance such bits of white space signify when he writes: ". . . in the universe Auschwitz, everything is mystery. . . . White spaces themselves have their importance." Clear evidence of this abounds in this true story.

The theme of silence found in *Night*, however, extends far beyond such textual elements of words and blanks. If this testimony represents the absolute negative pole attainable by silence, we must undertake to seek out its cancerous growth within other elements as they are drawn into the vortex of the evil. The primary level at which one discovers this negative silence is the utter destruction of the self. "Silence in its primal aspect, is a consequence of terror, of a dissolution of self and world that, once known, can never be fully dispelled." This loss of identity effectively silences the image that constitutes human essence. [As writer Victor Frankl explains], "One literally became a number: dead or alive that was unimportant; the life of a number was completely irrelevant." This destruction extends beyond simple identity as it seeks to silence the unique world of childhood and innocence. One must therefore seek to trace the evolution of the antithesis of all human values, in general, and the Jewish ethos, in particular, an action that is achieved by a painful silencing of words by words as readers are conducted into the chaos of silent, destructive negativity. Proceeding a step beyond, one must subsequently seek the ultimate denial of God, humanity, and the word in order to arrive at the heart of the Holocaust.

The first element of life that must be silenced is time. Time lies at the heart of existence, a principle particularly true in Jewish thought and teachings. Abraham Joshua Heschel notes that "Judaism is a religion of time aiming at the sancti-fication of time." So it is that at the beginning of *Night*, time meticulously and meaningfully guides the young protagonist through life, through his studies and prayers. Time is repre-sented as a creative force, a bridge linking man to eternity.

The first incursion of night into the harmonious passage of time is the deportation and subsequent return of Moshe the Beadle. The destructive silence of the Jewish tragedy has taken its toll. . . . "He closed his eyes, as though to escape time" (*Night*, 17). More importantly, this silencing of time brings with it other startling transformations. . . . "Moshe had changed. There was no longer any joy in his eyes. He no longer sang. He no longer talked to me of God or the cab-bala." As time is silenced, creativity ceases, and negative si-lence descends over life.

Moshe's return not only marks the initial transformation of time, but it evokes a curious response from the Jewish community of Sighet. Moshe (whose name is Moses), the prophet who has seen the advancing night, is viewed as be-ing a madman. The Jews would prefer to purchase his si-lence, to erase his message. Ironically, Moshe's purchased mutism only permits the Jews of Sighet to resume life be-hind a protective facade of silence that descends. But this brief contact with the night has unquestionably altered life. Though the Allied broadcasts offer a degree of hope, Wiesel underlies the text with a bitter irony: The utter silence of the Allies concerning the fate of Europe's Jewish population.

Though metamorphosing, time persists in its existence. With its natural passage the Nazis arrive. The course which would lead to Birkenau has been set into motion. Ghettos were established where life sought to maintain a degree of normalcy. Stories, part of the fabric of Jewish life, continued to be told. But, in the middle of things, the good stories being told are silenced and will remain forever unfinished. Words have lost their positive creative powers. The only remaining significant communication becomes nonverbal. Whereas time had previously stimulated creativity, it now stifles the word/Word. Time comes to represent a negative force, and even the "ongoing tale" is tainted by it.

Religious traditions whose foundations rest on the posi-tive nature of time are effectively altered. . . . "We had the traditional Friday evening meal. We said the customary grace for the bread and wine and swallowed our food without a word." The traditional Jewish Sabbath meal, which inaugurates the day of rest, is a time of joy and song. The table is literally considered an altar to God around which special Sabbath songs, *zmirot,* are sung. Family and friends join together in peace and speak of God, the Sabbath, and the joys of life. These elements are pointedly absent. . . .

Wiesel's use of the Sabbath in this context is essential, for if the silencing of time is to be absolute, the element of *kdusha* (holiness), which first appears in the Bible with reference to time—"And God blessed the seventh day and made it holy" (Genesis 2:3)—must be removed. Holiness is lodged in time, most notably on one particular day: the Sabbath. . . . As the final blow, therefore, the Sabbath, replete with its holiness, is silenced. . . . "Saturday, the day of rest, was chosen for our expulsion." The synagogue where Sabbath prayers had previously been offered is transformed into a scene of desecration. . . .

> The synagogue was like a huge station. . . . The altar was broken, the hangings torn down, the walls bare. There were so many of us that we could scarcely breathe. We spent a horrible twenty-four hours there. There were men downstairs; women on the first floor. It was Saturday; it was as though we had come to attend the service. Since no one could go out, people were relieving themselves in a corner.

Not only has the Sabbath been stilled, but with this act of unholiness, universal *menuhah* (rest; repose) has been destroyed. In the ensuing timeless silent void, there is no place for the Jews of Sighet.

The final rupture of time occurs with the arrival of the deported Jews at Birkenau-Auschwitz. After a seemingly endless night in the stinking confines of the cattle cars, time ceases to exist as they enter the kingdom of night where all the imagined horrors of two millennia of Christian iconography become real.

> Not far from us, flames were leaping up from the ditch, gigantic flames. They were burning something. A lorry drew up at the pit and delivered its load—little children. Babies! Yes, I saw it—saw it with my own eyes . . . those children in the flames.

Such a vision cannot be real; it cannot exist within a normal temporal framework. . . ."I pinched my face. Was I still alive? Was I awake?" Moral time, creative time, that dimension in which humanity exists and in which it discovers traces of the living God has been abrogated. . . . "I had lost all sense of time. . . . Surely it was a dream." The coup de grace is finally dealt by the camp code of hairlessness. All vestiges of age disappear as young and old are reduced to naked, hairless beings. With the erasure of time, little remains of the protagonist.

This argument has merely attempted to point to the silencing of time within the Wieselian universe. In *Night*, time ceases to have a creative dimension and enters the realm of pure negativism. As Wiesel's work evolves, time will remain fragmented as he passes from the world of the living to the domain of the dead. This particular feature produces a unique literary structure that will facilitate the blending of the past, present, and future, and will reinforce the notion of the instantaneous multiplicity of various levels of perception and significance. . . .

As time is closely related to our understanding of reality, its silencing must therefore effect the existence and perception of truth. As previously noted, when Moshe the Beadle returned from his deportation and sought to warn the Jews of Sighet about the existence of the concentration camp, no one would believe him. His vision of truth could not be accommodated within a traditional temporal framework. This attitude is strengthened when, during the journey to Auschwitz, Moshe's words are echoed and even intensified in the frightening prophetic ravings of Mme. Schächter.

Within the timeless world of the sealed cattle cars that serve as the bridge between Sighet and Auschwitz, between life and death, the journey becomes a metonymy of existence in the concentration camp. In this environment, Mme. Schächter's voice painfully reiterates the horrific reality Moshe's had announced earlier, and which their current journey represents. The others react to her much as they had to Moshe: They attempt to silence her. Nothing, however, is capable of stifling her violent, prophetic outbursts. . . .

Eliezer has come to exist within a timeless void from which truth has been either exiled or deformed. In this silent wasteland, he will suffer the destruction of his own beliefs in a just and true God, as well as in the goodness of fellow human beings. Wiesel accomplishes this annihilation of Eliezer's essence within the space of seventeen pages as the devouring black flame of the concentration camp rapidly erases the being who had existed. Within the text, silence becomes the method by which Eliezer is reduced to a cipher.

This silence is evoked by several techniques. Sparse dialogue couples with terse, journalistic language, and long pauses to create a taut, fearful atmosphere. The word *silence* and its synonyms do not recur frequently, a choice that saves them from becoming meaningless clichés. Wiesel does, however, strike upon another technique: Punctuation. The use of punctuation accentuates the rapid respiration of the text and creates a feeling of impending doom. The text progresses haltingly, tripping and failing on its descent to hell.

Another striking feature is the absolute lack of gruesome detail, or even the mention of death. For the reader, these elements exist, but only in the meta-silence that Wiesel imposes and which forms the background of the story. The language of the concentration camp is one which cannot be expressed in common terms.... Wiesel does relegate certain realities of the concentration camp to silence. And yet, unexpressed elements do eventually rise from the depths to extinguish the voices of the living.

[Scholar] Roland Barthes believes that the voice is the symbolic substance of human life. As a symbol of life, the voice has no rightful place in the kingdom of death and is therefore methodically silenced. First, the protagonist's father's voice is stilled, then Eliezer's. Gradually, language itself is silenced. Life as it has been perceived ceases to exist.

With time and creative language silenced, the spirit of the concentration camp proceeds to invade Eliezer's soul and crushes his spiritual identity. One of the most painful acts is the demolition of the protagonist's view of God. The young talmudic student deeply believed in God, and had always nurtured the notion of the unique convenantal relationship between the Jews and God. Man would supplicate; God would respond. To those faced with the reality of Auschwitz, God reveals Himself as an impotent entity who has been robbed of His attributes of justice and mercy by the Angel of Death. For Wiesel, the God of the yeshiva student has abdicated His Throne.

The pious Jew prays three times daily. During the morning prayers, psalms are chanted to the Creator of the Universe. Within the horrific kingdom of night such psalms would prove to be ironically blasphemous or utterly senseless. So it is that Wiesel composes a new psalm, one which reflects the negativity of Auschwitz and the eclipse of God. ... This striking text similarly signifies the protagonist's utter disillusionment with God. Former beliefs possess no va-lidity. Eliezer has found that his God is lost amid the negative silence of the concentration camp. And God's own silence amid such incarnate evil indicts and condemns Him. Yet despite such a challenge to his beliefs, Eliezer never rejects the existence of God. The silence of Auschwitz has submitted the omnipotent God of Eliezer's youth to the test of truth, only to find Him wanting.

Not only is God called to the bar in this silence; the very notion of humanity, the enlightened being to which Mauriac makes reference in his Preface to the novel, is likewise examined and found to be wanting. The vision of the human race has radically altered. On "planet Auschwitz," human moral responsibilities are silenced and deformed into indifference. Humankind blindly and mutely accepts the events of the Holocaust. Human guilt is first evidenced while the Jews of Sighet are still in their ghetto. The "others" in the town indifferently accept matters, and eventually witness the deportation of their Jewish neighbors. Their silence condemns them and, by extension, all humanity. . . . The very fact that the Jewish population could so easily be deported destroys Eliezer's innocent illusions about human goodness and justice. Thus, for the protagonist, the corrosive, negative mentality of the concentration camp philosophy, that of every person for himself/herself and every person being your enemy, evolves and assumes primacy. The view of humanity, created in the image of God, is shattered and banished. The last shreds of respectful human dignity fall away under the cries of camp guards. The ultimate silencing blow to human identity occurs when Eliezer is stripped of his name and thereafter becomes A-7713.

By the conclusion of this third episode, the silent backdrop of Auschwitz has annihilated the voices of the pre-Holocaust world. The remainder of the narrative merely serves to supplement this initial silencing. The voice that is bound up with life and in life is strangled and muted. Only the chaotic, destructive silence of the evil remains.

Each of the various episodes comprising the story of *Night* reflects the omnipresent scenic silence of Auschwitz. Wiesel's use of the morphological, syntactic, and semantic aspects of silence permit the novel to descend into the depths of depraved negativity. And the principal question raised by the theme of silence emerges as: Where was God?

This becomes the central issue about which silence and all other themes come to revolve.

In the opening episodes, Eliezer had been transported from the light of learning and truth to the blackness of the void as experienced at Auschwitz. Prayer and praise were cut off before a silent God. The only force to which one could respond, the only source of potency, were the Nazis. . . . Each step, every example, emphasizes the absence of the divine and the presence of evil. Akiba Drumer, another character whose faith is shattered, poses this most serious question: "Where is God?" Those three words, like the four opening notes of Beethoven's Fifth Symphony, pound out the single most urgent question against which Eliezer and all humanity must struggle. Where was God? At the public hanging of a young boy that obsessive question arises from the meta-silence before uneasily dissolving again into it:

"Where is God now?"
And I heard a voice within me answer him:
"Where is He? Here He is—He is hanging here on this
    gallows. . . ."

This particular scene reflects the final silencing of the young protagonist's faith and hopes in the God of his youth. The powerful God of his religious studies possesses no meaning in Auschwitz. How could one maintain belief in the majesty and justice of God in the face of such debasement and depravity? The overwhelming silence of God generates a spiritual revolt within Eliezer, so that on Rosh Hashana, he refuses to pray or to bless God's Name. God stands in the dock, accused by Eliezer of silent indifference. This rebellion casts the protagonist into the depths of a void where he is painfully alone in a world whence God has been exiled. This bitter estrangement culminates ten days later on Yom Kippur when Eliezer abandons the obligatory fast and stresses: "I no longer accepted God's silence."

As Eliezer no longer possesses faith in God, he must seek strength and life elsewhere. In the context of traditional Jewish life, such a source of comfort and renewal can be found within the family. Yet the family unit Eliezer had known was forever ruptured upon his arrival in the concentration camp when his mother and sisters had been marched off to the gas chambers. His only hope lies in his father whose hand he tightly holds. . . .

But his father's voice, that had come to signify life, is gradually silenced. Without his voice, Eliezer's father effectively no longer exists in this world. The child assumes the role of father, the father the child. And yet, even as his father weakens, even as their relationship together is gradually silenced—a relationship that represents the last vestige of Eliezer's Jewishness—the protagonist refuses to abandon his father. . . . Unable to cry when his father dies, Eliezer has but one thought: Free at last! Death has silenced his only link with the past, with the family, with tradition.

The path that Eliezer has trod with his father is now his alone. His father, his God, his world, are dead. This is his inheritance. "In *Night* I wanted to show the end, the finality of the event. Everything came to an end—man, history, literature, religion, God. There was nothing left." So it is that the protagonist has been swallowed by the silent void of Auschwitz. . . . "From the depths of the mirror, a corpse gazed back at me.". . . Eliezer will always exist in a realm of ghosts. The cadaverous gaze in the mirror at Buchenwald reflects the paralyzed, mute victim perfectly.

CHAPTER 2

The Art of *Night*

READINGS ON *NIGHT*

More Questions than Answers

Benj Mahle

Benj Mahle, an English teacher at Frank B. Kellogg Junior High in Rochester, Minnesota, was initially frustrated at not being able to answer the questions *Night* raised about the Holocaust. How could the Germans have done it? Why didn't the Jews listen to warnings? Mahle deduced that Wiesel knows there are no easy answers to the events that took place, and purposefully left many things open for interpretation. He believes that it is in the very questioning itself that one begins to feel the anguish that the prisoners experienced; and that trying to find the answers to the past will bring hope for the future.

In teaching *Night*, Elie Wiesel's puissant and often poetic account of his Holocaust experiences, I used to feel a gnawing inadequacy when my ninth grade students would ask questions for which I had no satisfactory responses. "Why," they'd ask, "did the Jews of Sighet not believe Moche the Beadle when he described to them the details of the pogrom he had miraculously survived?" Or, "How could the Nazis dump a truck load of babies into a burning pit, and feel nothing? How could a son attack and kill his own father for a mouthful of bread? How could anyone survive a forty mile march through the freezing night with only snow to eat?" Only recently have I become comfortable with answering "I don't know" or "I'm not sure" when they confront me with questions like those.

This change results from my latest rereading of *Night* wherein I've concluded that Elie Wiesel intended his account to be ambiguous, that he hoped to raise more questions than he would answer.

For example, consider his treatment of the theme of religious faith. In chapter three, the young Elie—heretofore a profound believer—first experiences the atrocities of the Auschwitz camp. Subsequently he declares, "Never shall I forget those flames which consumed my faith forever." *Consumed* suggests total destruction. Yet there are subtle suggestions that at least a flicker of faith remains. For as he details the horrors being perpetrated by men, he consistently contrasts these with benign, even appealing images of nature. Since we frequently perceive nature as a reflection of God, is it not possible to interpret these images as evidence of God's concern? In this passage Elie is being moved to a new camp (the italics are mine):

> Ten gypsies had come and joined our supervisor. Whips and truncheons cracked around me. My feet were running without my being aware of it. I tried to hide from the blows behind the others. *The spring sunshine . . .*

Later,

> The gypsies stopped near another barracks. They were replaced by SS, who surrounded us. Revolvers, machine guns, police dogs. The march had lasted half an hour. Looking around me I noticed that the barbed wires were behind us. We had left camp.
>
> *It was a beautiful April day, the fragrance of spring was in the air. The sun was setting in the west.*
>
> But we had been marching for only a few moments when we saw the barbed wire of another camp. An iron door with the inscription over it: "Work is Liberty"—Auschwitz.

These references to the natural beauty of this day may give support to the notion that God is offering hope. On the other hand, perhaps the author is sarcastically suggesting that God merely deigned to ease their suffering by allowing that it should be done in pleasant weather. Consider another passage from chapter three—Elie's moving and deeply poetic description of his first night in camp:

> Never shall I forget that night, the first night in camp, which has turned my life into one long night, seven times cursed and seven times sealed. Never shall I forget that smoke. Never shall I forget the little faces of the children, whose bodies I saw turned into wreaths of smoke beneath a *silent blue sky.*

Few things in nature stir in us more hope for a fine day that blue skies. Yet I wonder if the contrast here is supposed to provide a suggestion of hope? Is it instead a quiet condemnation of God's apparent silence, represented by the

A POEM ABOUT TEACHING *NIGHT*

Thomas E. Thorton, an English teacher in New York, struggles over using Night *to teach his young students about the Holocaust. He expresses his anguish in a poem published in* English Journal.

On Wiesel's *Night*
I cannot teach this book. Instead,
I drop copies on their desks,
like bombs on sleeping towns,
and let them read. So do I, again.
The stench rises from the page
and chokes my throat.
The ghosts of burning babies
haunt my eyes.
And that bouncing baton,
that pointer of Death,
stabs me in the heart
as it sends his mother
to the blackening sky.
Nothing is destroyed
the laws of science say,
only changed.
The millions transformed into
precious smoke ride the wind
to fill our lungs and hearts
with their cries.

No, I cannot teach this book.
I simply want the words
to burn their comfortable souls
and leave them scarred for life.
                    Thomas E. Thorton
                    East Greenbrush, New York

Thomas E. Thorton, "On Wiesel's *Night*", *English Journal*, vol. 79, no. 2, February 1990, p. 87.

tranquility of nature at a moment when it would seem right that a sudden tempest should douse the flames or the earth should open up and swallow the murderers? Elie Wiesel consistently provides readers with details rather than explanations. And I believe his purpose in providing these contrasting images is appropriately ambiguous.

In the first pages of his book, the author states that his teacher, Moche the Beadle, believed that "every question possessed a power that did not lie in the answer." The questions posed by my students during their reading of *Night* evince a power that has moved many of them to seek more information. Ultimately, in attempting to find their own answers, these students experience shock and revulsion that in the entire history of the human race such questions should ever have needed to be asked. Their curiosity and the complexity of the issues forces them to experience the power of these questions with their hearts as well as their heads.

So, I no longer feel frustration when I don't satisfy the curiosities of my students during their study of *Night* and the Holocaust. For I've concluded that what is important is *not* that all these questions should be answered; what is important is that all of us should continue to ask them. I believe it was to this end that Elie Wiesel created a *poetic* account of awful beauty, ambiguity, and power. He must have sensed that as long as we question the events of the Holocaust, our memory of it—and our outrage—will be an eternal flame within each of us.

Facing the Horror of History

Lea Hamaoui

Lea Hamaoui, a professor at Baruch College in Brook-
lyn, acknowledges how difficult it is for any writer to
truly capture the essence of history. This is particularly evident in the case of the Holocaust, when readers want to believe that such horrors didn't really take
place. She explores the methods Wiesel uses in *Night*
to lure the reader so deeply into the story that by the
end of it the horror is undeniably real.

To render historical horror is to render, by definition, that
which exceeds rendering; it projects pain for which there is
no solace, no larger consolation, no redemptive possibility. . . .
The young Eliezer staring into the mirror upon his liberation
from Buchenwald has gained knowledge, but this knowledge
in no way justifies the sufferings that preceded it. It is not a
sign of positive spiritual development. Nor is it linked to
restorative changes in the moral and political realm. *Night* is
not about a moral political order violated and restored, but
about the shattering of the idea of such an order. . . .

Night proceeds from experience that is not universal. It
does not expand from kernels of the familiar but from the
unfamiliar, from data in historical reality. The deaths of
Eliezer's father, of Akiva Drummer, of Juliek the violinist
and of Meir Katz are different because, after all of the pain,
there is nothing to be extracted by way of compensation.
They are not symbolic but very real, and we experience not
a purging of feelings tapped but the fear of the unpredictable
in life to which we, like the Jews of *Night*, are subject.

If symbol is something that stands in place of something
else, the historical narrative does not stand in place of our
experience, but alongside it. We experience historical narrative much the way we experience a neighbor's report of his

Excerpted from "Historical Horror and the Shape of *Night*," by Lea Hamaoui, in *Elie
Wiesel: Between Memory and Hope*, edited by Carol Rittner (New York: New York University Press, 1990). Reprinted by permission of Carol Rittner.

or her visit to a place we have not ourselves visited. The report is informational—it is "adjacent" to our experience, neither interpretive nor metaphorical nor symbolic. It is "other" than our experience but also part of the same historical matrix within which we experience the flow of our own lives. *Night* threatens and disturbs in a way that symbolic narrative does not.

Night is Wiesel's attempt to bring word of the death camps back to humanity in such a form that his message, unlike that of Moshe the Beadle to Eliezer and to the Jews of Sighet, will not be rejected. The word I wish to stress here is *form.* The work, which is eyewitness account, is also much more than eyewitness account. In its rhetorical and aesthetic design, *Night* is shaped by the problematic of historical horror and by the resistances, both psychic and formal, to the knowledge Wiesel would convey.

When the narrator, Eliezer, sees a truck filled with children who are dumped into a fiery ditch, he cannot believe what he has seen: "I pinched my face. Was I alive? Was I awake? I could not believe it. How could it be possible for them to burn people, children, and for the world to keep silent? No, none of this could be true. It was a nightmare."

Eliezer cannot believe what is before his eyes. His disbelief seems to numb him physically—he pinches his face to ascertain that the medium of that vision, his body, is alive, perceiving, present. So fundamental is the horror to which he is an eyewitness that seeing comes at the expense of his bodily awareness of himself as a vital and perceiving entity. What Eliezer witnesses contradicts psychic underpinnings of existence so thoroughly that his very awareness brings with it feelings of deadness.

It is precisely this moment, this confrontation with data that negates the human impulses and ideas that structure our lives, with which Wiesel is concerned. We cannot know that which we cannot know. In order to bring the fact of Auschwitz to us, Wiesel must deal with the inherent difficulty of assimilating the truth he would portray.

His method is simple, brilliant and depends upon a series of repetitions in which what is at stake is a breakdown of critical illusions. At this level, the experience of the reader reading the narrative is structurally parallel to his experience of life, at least as Karl Popper describes it. Life, in Popper's view, resembles the experience of a blind person who runs into an obstacle and thereby experiences its existence. Through the falsification of our assumptions we actually make contact with "reality." The refutation of our errors is the positive experience we gain from reality.

THROUGH ROSE-COLORED GLASSES

Eliezer's tale is the story of a series of shattered expectations, his and our own. The repetition of this "disappointment," of optimism proven hollow and warnings rejected, becomes the crucial aesthetic fact or condition within which we then experience the narrator's account of his experiences in Auschwitz, in Buna, in Gleiwitz, and in Buchenwald. In this way we come to experience the account of the death camps as an account cleansed of past illusion, pristine in its terrible truth.

The quest for this truth is established at the outset of the narrative in the figure of Moshe the Beadle. Eliezer is devoted to his studies of Talmud. His decision to study Kabbalah with Moshe focuses the narrative on the problematic of reality and imbues it with the spiritual longings of this quest.

> There are a thousand and one gates leading into the orchard of mystical truth. Every human being has his own gate . . .

> And Moshe the Beadle, the poor barefoot of Sighet, talked to me for long hours of the revelations and mysteries of the cabbala. It was with him that my initiation began. We would read together, ten times over, the same page of the Zohar. Not to learn it by heart, but to extract the divine essence from it.

> And throughout those evenings a conviction grew in me that Moshe the Beadle would draw me with him into eternity, into that time where question and answer would become one.

The book, which begins with Eliezer's search for a teacher of mystical knowledge and ends with Eliezer's contemplating his image in a mirror after his liberation from Buchenwald, proposes a search for ultimate knowledge in terms that are traditional, while the knowledge it offers consists of data that is historical, radical, and subversive.

If directionality of the narrative is established early, a counter-direction makes itself felt very quickly. Following Eliezer's dream of a formal harmony, eternity and oneness toward which Moshe would take him, Eliezer's initiation into the "real" begins:

Then one day they expelled all the foreign Jews from Sighet.
And Moshe the Beadle was a foreigner.

Crammed into cattle trains by Hungarian police, they wept
bitterly. We stood on the platform and wept too.

Moshe is shot but escapes from a mass grave in one of the
Galician forests of Poland near Kolomaye and returns to
Sighet in order to warn the Jews there. He describes children used as targets for machine guns and the fate of a
neighbor, Malka, and of Tobias the tailor.

From this point onward in the narrative, a powerful
counter-direction of flight away from truth, knowledge, reality, and history is set into motion. Moshe is not believed, not
even by his disciple, Eliezer. The Jews of Sighet resist the
news Moshe has brought them:

I wanted to come back to Sighet to tell you the story of my
death . . . And see how it is, no one will listen to me . . .

And we, the Jews of Sighet, were waiting for better days,
which would not be long in coming now.

Yes, we even doubted that he [Hitler] wanted to exterminate
us.

Was he going to wipe out a whole people? Could he exterminate a population scattered throughout so many countries?
So many millions! What method could he use? And in the
middle of the twentieth century?

RESISTING THE NEW REALITY

Optimism persists with the arrival of the Germans. After
Sighet is divided into a big and little ghetto, Wiesel writes,
"little by little life returned to normal. The barbed wire
which fenced us in did not cause us any real fear."

While the narrative presses simultaneously toward and
away from the "real," the real events befalling the Jews of
Sighet are perceived as unreal:

On everyone's back was a pack. . . . Here came the Rabbi, his
back bent, his face shaved, his pack on his back. His mere
presence among the deportees added a touch of unreality to
the scene. It was like a page torn from some story book, from
some historical novel about the captivity of Babylon or the
Spanish Inquisition.

The intensity of the resistance peaks in the boxcar in
which, Eliezer and his family are taken to the death camp.
Madame Schächter, distraught by the separation from her

pious husband and two older sons, has visions of fire: "Jews, listen to me! I can see a fire! There are huge flames! It is a furnace!" Her words prey on nerves, fan fears, dispel illusion: "We felt that an abyss was about to open beneath our bodies." She is gagged and beaten. As her cries are silenced the chimneys of Auschwitz come into view:

> We had forgotten the existence of Madame Schächter. Suddenly we heard terrible screams: Jews, look! Look through the window! Flames! Look!
>
> And as the train stopped, we saw this time that flames were gushing out of a tall chimney into the black sky.

The movement toward and away from the knowledge of historical horror that Moshe the Beadle brings back from the mass grave and the violence that erupts when precious illusions are disturbed, shapes the narrative of *Night*. The portrait and analysis of the resistances to knowing help situate the reader in relation to the historical narrative and imbue the narrative with the felt historicity of the world outside the book. Eliezer's rejection of the knowledge that Moshe brings back, literally, from the grave, predicts our own rejection of that knowledge. His failure to believe the witness prepares the reader for the reception of Eliezer's own story of his experience in Auschwitz by first examining the defenses that Eliezer, and, thereby, implicitly, the reader, would bring to descriptions of Auschwitz. The rejection of Moshe strips the reader of his own deafness in advance of the arrival at Auschwitz.

EYES WIDE OPEN

Once stripped of his defenses, the reader moves from a fortified, to an open, undefended position vis-à-vis the impact of the narrative. Because the lines between narrative art and life have been erased, Wiesel brings the reader into an existential relationship to the historical experience recounted in *Night*. By virtue of that relationship, the reader is transformed into a witness. The act of witnessing is ongoing for most of the narrative, a narrative that is rife with horror and with the formal dissonances that historically experienced horror must inflict upon language.

Human extremity challenges all formal representation of it. It brings the world of language and the world outside language into the uncomfortable position of two adjacent notes

THE BURDEN OF THE DEAD

In Confronting the Holocaust: The Impact of Elie Wiesel, *English professor and author Lawrence L. Langer contemplates the burden that the dead continue to bestow upon Wiesel and on all of us.*

The compelling fact is that the millions of people [murdered in the Holocaust] are *not* gone, they haunt the writer with a ghostly persistence that casts a shadow on the imagination and leaves a disfiguring scar on the characters who populate his literary world. The imagination contending with the Holocaust is never free to create an independent reality; it is circumscribed by the literal event, by the history of the horror, by the sheer mass of anonymous dead who impose a special responsibility on the writer's talent. That burden is one feature of the altered consciousness that our age requires of us. The spirit of tragedy cannot absorb these dead; neither time nor history will silence their wail. . . . They present us with the dismal image of men dying for nothing.

This is a bizarre challenge for a reader nurtured on life, hope, and the future. . . . We all know the final lines from Elie Wiesel's first, and still one of his finest works, *Night:* "From the depths of the mirror, a corpse gazed back at me. The look in his eyes, as they stared back into mine, has never left me." Multiply that corpse a hundred, a thousand, a millionfold, and we will understand more clearly what is implied when we are told [by Holo-

on a piano keyboard that are simultaneously pressed and held. The sounds they produce jar the ear. In a work of historical horror, language and life, expression and experience are perceived as separate opaque structures, each of which is inadequate to encompass the abyss that separates them.

The most powerful passages in *Night* are those that mark Eliezer's arrival in Auschwitz. The family is separated. Eliezer and his father go through a selection and manage to stay together. Eliezer watches a truck drop living children into a ditch full of flames. He and his father conclude that this is to be Eliezer's fate as well. Eliezer decides he will run into an electrified wire fence and electrocute himself rather than face an excruciating death in the flaming ditch.

The moment is extraordinary and extreme beyond the wildest of human imaginings. Hearing his fellow Jews murmur the Kaddish, a formula of praise of the Almighty that is the traditional prayer for the dead, Eliezer revolts: "For the caust scholar Alvin Rosenfeld] that because of the Holocaust, "the imagination has come to one of its periodic endings and stands at the threshold of new and more difficult beginnings."

The burden of the dead, of *such* dead, which the Holocaust has bequeathed to us and which is present on nearly every page Elie Wiesel has written, was anticipated before the invention of the extermination camp. In an essay unpretentiously called "Thoughts for the Times on War and Death," published in 1915 shortly after the outbreak of World War I, Sigmund Freud recognized how a conflict of such dimensions would disfigure conventional assumptions about dying. We "cannot maintain our former attitude towards death," Freud insisted, "and we have not yet discovered a new one." Thirty years later the Holocaust confirmed Freud's intuition, for he had also argued that until men found a way of absorbing into their cultural assumptions the phenomenon of mass dying for no justifiable reason, they would continue to live psychologically beyond their means. One of the main problems of the Holocaust writer is to find a secure place, somewhere between memory and imagination, for all those corpses who, like the ghost of Hamlet's father, cry out against the injustice of their end, but for whom no act of vengeance or ritual of remembrance exists sufficient to bring them to a peaceful place of rest.

Alvin H. Rosenfeld and Irving Greenberg, eds., "The Divided Voice," in *Confronting the Holocaust: The Impact of Elie Wiesel*, Bloomington: Indiana University Press, 1978.

first time, I felt revolt rise up in me. Why should I bless His name? The Eternal Lord of the Universe, the All-Powerful and Terrible, was silent. What had I to thank Him for?" The Jews continue their march and Eliezer begins to count the steps before he will jump at the wire:

> Ten steps still. Eight. Seven. We marched slowly on, as though following a hearse at our own funeral . . . There it was now, right in front of us, the pit and its flames. I gathered all that was left of my strength, so that I could break from the ranks and throw myself upon the barbed wire. In the depths of my heart, I bade farewell to my father, to the whole universe.

And the words of the Kaddish, hallowed by centuries and disavowed only moments before, words of praise and of affirmation of divine oneness, spring unbidden to his lips: "and in spite of myself, the words formed themselves and issued in a whisper from my lips: *Yitgadal veyitkadach shme raba* . . . May His name be blessed and magnified." Eliezer does not run to the wire. The entire group turns left and enters a barracks.

The question of formal dissonance in *Night is* revealing. The narrative that would represent historical horror works, finally, against the grain of the reader and of the psychic structures that demand the acknowledgments, resolutions, closure, equivalence, and balances. . . .

The words of the Kaddish in *Night* do not express the horror to which Eliezer is a witness. They flow from an inner necessity and do not reflect but deflect that horror. They project the sacredness of life in the face of its most wrenching desecration. They affirm life at the necessary price of disaffirming the surrounding reality. The world of experience and the world of language could not, at this moment, be further apart. Experience is entirely beyond words. Words are utterly inadequate to convey experience.

NEVER FORGET

The dissonance makes itself felt stylistically as well. Eliezer sums up his response to these first shattering hours of his arrival at Auschwitz in the most famous passages of *Night* and, perhaps, of all of Wiesel's writing: "Never shall I forget that night, the first night in camp, which has turned my life into one long night, seven times cursed and seven times sealed." The passage takes the form of an oath never to forget this night of his arrival. The oath, the recourse to metaphorical language ("which has turned my life into one long night"), the reference to curses and phraseology ("seven times cursed") echo the biblical language in which Eliezer was so steeped. He continues: "Never shall I forget that smoke. Never shall I forget the little faces of the children, whose bodies I saw turned into wreaths of smoke beneath a silent blue sky." The oath is an oath of protest, the "silent blue sky," an accusation: "Never shall I forget those flames which consumed my faith forever." Here and in the sentences that follow, Wiesel uses the rhythms, the verbal energy, imagery, and conventions of the Bible to challenge, accuse, and deny God:

> Never shall I forget that nocturnal silence which deprived me, for all eternity, of the desire to live. Never shall I forget those moments which murdered my God and my soul and turned my dreams to dust. Never shall I forget these things, even if I am condemned to live as long as God Himself. Never.

The elaborate oath of remembrance recalls the stern biblical admonitions of remembrance. The negative formulation of the oath and the incremental repetition of the word "never" register defiance and anger even as the eight repetitions circumscribing the passage give it rhythmic structure and ceremonial shape. Ironically, these repetitions seem to implicate mystical notions of God's covenant with the Jews, a covenant associated with the number eight because the ceremony of entrance into the covenant by way of circumcision takes place on the eighth day after birth. The passage uses the poetry and language of faith to affirm a shattering of faith.

The passage is a tour de force of contradiction, paradox, and formal dissonances that are not reconciled, but juxtaposed and held up for inspection. In a sparely written, tightly constructed narrative, it is the only extended poetic moment. It is a climactic moment, and, strangely, for a work that privileges a world outside words altogether, a rhetorical moment: a moment constructed out of words and the special effects and properties of their combinations, a moment that hovers above the abyss of human extremity in uncertain relationship to it.

Like the taste of bread to a man who has not eaten, the effect of so poetic a passage lies in what preceded it. Extremity fills words with special and different meanings. Eliezer reacts to the words of one particular SS officer: "But his clipped words made us tremble. Here the word 'furnace' was not a word empty of meaning; it floated on the air, mingling with the smoke. It was perhaps the only word which did have any real meaning here."

THE REAL NIGHT

Wiesel's narrative changes our conventional sense of the word "night" in the course of our reading. Night, which as a metaphor for evil always projects, however subliminally, the larger rhythm and structure within which the damages of evil are mitigated, comes to stand for another possibility altogether. The word comes to be filled with the historical flames and data for which there are no metaphors, no ameliorating or sublimating structures. It acquires the almost-tactile feel of the existential, opaque world that is the world of the narrative and also the world in which we live.

Perhaps the finest tribute to *Night* is to be found in the

prologue of Terrence Des Pres's book on poetry and politics, *Praises and Dispraises.* Des Pres is speaking of Czeslaw Milosz and of other poets who have lived through extremity and writes: "If we should wonder why their voices are valued so highly, it's that they are acquainted with the night, the nightmare spectacle of politics especially." Des Pres uses the word "night" and the reader immediately understands it in exactly Wiesel's revised sense of it.

To be acquainted with the night, in this sense, and to bring that knowledge to a readership is to bring the world we live in into sharper focus. The necessary job of making a better world cannot possibly begin from anywhere else.

Christian Imagery

Michael Brown

Michael Brown, a professor of humanities and language studies in Toronto, fears that the Christian symbolism Wiesel incorporates into *Night* might be misinterpreted. It may lead the reader to believe that Wiesel is turning his back on Judaism, as in fact some Jews did following the Holocaust. Through close analysis of *Night* and Wiesel's intentions, he asserts that Wiesel's motives may have been to show not only how difficult it is for Jews to keep their faith after the Holocaust, but also that since Christianity was the main faith of those who committed the acts of atrocity in the first place, it ought to be difficult being Christian as well.

However much one might regret it, few can fail to sympathize with, and even to participate in, the theological questioning which the Holocaust has sparked. The survivors—and, in a sense, we are all survivors—need ways of understanding. Yet the explanations which past generations have offered for Jewish suffering do not satisfy. Some Jews have been relatively unaffected, but others have lost their belief in God entirely and not regained it. Still others see the Holocaust as the symbol of God's ultimate rejection of Judaism and have become Christian. Rabbi Elisha ben Abuyah, the Talmud relates, foreswore belief in God after witnessing the death of only one innocent child. One cannot but understand if faith breaks after having witnessed the death of six million innocent men, women and children. . . .

The conversion of Jews to Christianity as a response to the Holocaust seems all the more ignoble in the light of the traditional Christian explanation of Jewish suffering. Christians have understood that suffering to be divine punishment for the Jews' twofold sin, first, of failing to recognize the divinity and Messiahship of Jesus and then, according to

Excerpted from "On Crucifying the Jews," by Michael Brown, *Judaism*, vol. 27, no. 4, Fall 1978. Reprinted with permission from the American Jewish Congress.

the classical reading of history, of causing his death. The sins of the Jewish parents are to be visited upon their children: Jews for all time are punished for the blindness and cruelty of their ancestors. Their permanent downcast state serves as witness to the truth of Christianity. . . .

Some Christians still adhere to the traditional doctrine regarding Jewish suffering and understand the Holocaust as one more manifestation of the wrath of God being visited upon the Jews for their 2000-years-ago sin. One can appreciate the desire of theological conservatives to see all events fitting into classical doctrine. Still, to an outsider, such an explanation seems unacceptable on its own terms. What kind of God would require the degradation, torture, and death of a million Jewish children in the twentieth century as atonement for the shortsightedness of their ancestors two millennia ago? How can anyone believe in such a deity?

Indeed, how can one account for the attraction of Jews to such a belief, especially since Christianity is the faith system, at least nominally, of the perpetrators of the Holocaust? Not surprisingly, many Jews respond with a special measure of distaste when faced with Holocaust survivors who have embraced Christianity. Incomprehension and discomfort are no less acute in confronting works of literature and art which use Christian myth and symbol to interpret the Holocaust.

In fact, Jewish writers who employ Christian terminology to write about the Holocaust have generally evoked dumbfounded consternation from Jewish critics. Elie Wiesel's *Night* . . . is one of the most widely read works of Holocaust literature, . . . yet the obvious Christian elements in these works have been ignored by critics who are either too embarrassed or are just uncomprehending. . . .

PLACING BLAME

Classical Judaism understood the destruction of the Temple, the subsequent exile, and most other tribulations of the Jews as punishment for their failure to achieve *tikkun olam bemalkhut shaddai,* the construction in Palestine of the ideal society revealed to them at Sinai and later by God himself, the society which was to serve as a model for the entire world. . . .

One might, of course, look upon the state of Israel as the rebirth of the "saving remnant." But it is hard to imagine that Judaism, which could not countenance the sacrifice of one man, Isaac, as a testimonial to faith, would consider six million human sacrifices, all of them unwilling, an appropriate means of bringing about the restoration of Jewish sovereignty.

But even if classical Judaism offers no acceptable mythological frame for interpreting the Holocaust, the use of Christian mythology should be out of bounds to Jews. The Cross is not a universal symbol of suffering; it is a very particular Christian mode of understanding experience. Judaism has different myths from Christianity and different values, although it shares a good many with it, especially those which originated in the Hebrew Bible. Jews cannot see Jewish experience—or any experience—in Christian terms and remain authentic Jews. To be themselves, Jews must express themselves in Jewish symbolic language, or, at the very least, in neutral language. When they opt for other symbols and myths, they can easily be seen to be rejecting Judaism and, indeed, may be doing so. This is especially the case with regard to Christian myth and symbol, because of the tension and competition which have almost always characterized the Christian-Jewish relationship.

Is it then the case that [Elie Wiesel has] ... sold out? Is their faith so broken that they have become closet Christians and now create entirely outside of the Jewish framework? The motivations of artists are not easily fathomed and the artists themselves are unlikely to be of assistance. Plato accused poets of not understanding their own poetry. In part, he was right. Robert Frost used to say that his job was to create poetry, while that of the readers was to understand it. But, while artists may be of little help in explaining their own works, the works themselves can sometimes be illuminating with regard to their creators. And, in fact, *Night*, ... and especially the way in which Christian imagery is used in [it does] ... yield some clues about the writer's motivation. ...

CRUCIFYING THE INNOCENT

This book, Wiesel's first and, to this reader, his most powerful work to date, is autobiographical, although apparently fictionalized to some extent. It is the tale of the journey from the sunny, imperturbable tranquility of a Transylvanian town into the nightmare of the concentration camps. It is the story of a father and his son, of their relationship which, alone, preserves the humanity of both and their will to live, and of the ultimate destruction of both humanity and the will to live by the Nazis' deliberate process of dehumanization.

In many ways *Night* is a very Jewish book. Its main characters, except for the Nazis and their collaborators, are all identifiably and positively Jewish. The narrator, Wiesel, is an aspiring young cabbalist when the book opens, and his father is one of the pillars of the Sighet Jewish establishment. When the Jews of Sighet are deported, the narrator sees the deportation in terms of the exile of the Jews to Babylon or, later, from Spain.

It is no surprise that in the hell of Birkenau many of the characters in the book—rabbis and laymen, including the narrator—lose their faith. God seems absent. In response, some people become defiant, although even their defiance is Jewish. (Wiesel, for instance, eats on Yom Kippur.) Others simply surrender their lives. Death becomes commonplace at Birkenau.

Two deaths, however, are not ordinary, and the narrator treats them rather differently from the others. The first is that of his friend, Akiba Drumer; and here there is introduced the Christian theme. Drumer bears the name of a great Jewish sage, a contemporary of Elisha ben Abuyah. Rabbi Akiba, however, kept faith in adversity. He sacrificed his life rather than obey the Roman prohibition against teaching Torah in Palestine. He died teaching others how to live by Torah, how to build the ideal world. Unlike his namesake of Roman times, Akiba Drumer, in his trials, loses faith in God. He cannot "see a proof of God in this Calvary." Like Jesus, in the Gospels of Matthew and Mark, Drumer predicts the hour of his own death and then dies, wondering, in the words of the Psalmist, why God has abandoned him.

The other extraordinary death is that of a beautiful child, a servant of one of the *kapos.* The narrator refers to the child, as do the other inmates, as "the little servant, the sad-eyed angel." In retribution for the sabotage activities of his boss, "the sad-eyed angel" is put to death, one of three people hanged together on a gallows. That there are three (two adults and one innocent child between them) suggests the Gospels' portrait of an innocent Jesus crucified together with two robbers, one on either side. The similarity with Jesus does not end there. Death does not come immediately to "the sad-eyed angel" when he is hanged, as it did not to Jesus. Suspended from the gallows, he dies slowly before the eyes of the unwilling onlookers. Then someone asks:

Where is God now?

The narrator responds to a voice within himself and answers:

Where is He? Here He is—He is hanging here on this gallows. . . .

In what is probably the climactic scene of *Night*, God dies on the gallows, just as Christians understand God to have done in the person of Jesus almost 2000 years ago.

Wiesel does not write of God rising. In François Mauriac's introduction to *Night*, however, an introduction to which Wiesel seems not to object, the Christian myth is completed. With unintended irony Mauriac asserts that, in modern Israel, "the Jewish nation has been resurrected from among its thousands of dead [millions!]," and that Wiesel himself physically resembles "that other Israeli, his brother, . . . the Crucified, whose Cross has conquered the world.". . .

No Glory Here

Since [Wiesel] . . . lived through the Holocaust in Hitler's Europe, . . . [he is], in fact, portraying [his] own [life] and experiences in Christian terms. The question remains: how is one to understand a Jew's having done so? . . .

In the opinion of this writer, . . . those who evince embarrassment at the Christian imagery of [*Night*], . . . fail altogether to grasp the significance of the work that they seek to interpret. To be sure, . . . Wiesel, . . . uses a Christian mythological frame and not a Jewish one. That, in itself, however, does not constitute evidence of wavering in the direction of a commitment to Christianity. Neither do the comments or behavior of the artist, which, as noted earlier, must always be taken with a grain of salt. . . .

Wiesel's non-Jews are not the focus of his book, and there are not many of them in it. He never identifies his gentiles as Christian, although they must be presumed to be at least nominally so, since they are Germans, Poles, and other Europeans. These Christians almost all serve as *kapos*, concentration camp authorities, Gestapo agents, or Hungarian or Roumanian police.

A few of them show some small degree of kindness to their Jewish victims. Most, however, as might be expected from what we know all too well about the camps, are brutish and brutal. They treat the Jews like animals; they are themselves predators and scavengers. There is not a single idealized or even admirable Christian in the book. Once, at a particularly difficult moment, the narrator hears a kind word from a young girl working in the camp. After the war he meets that same girl by accident in Paris. They reminisce. Finally, he summons the courage to ask; and, indeed, she turns out to be a Jew. The one kind non-prisoner with whom he had come in contact during all those long months was not a gentile, after all, but a Jew with Aryan papers. . . .

What emerges . . . , then, is, on the one hand, an approach to the Holocaust through Christian symbols and imagery, and, on the other hand, a portrait of Christians and their world as cruel and bestial. In that bestial society, the Jews suffer the fate of Jesus. They are crucified. It is the Christians who crucify them. . . . Jesus represents an ideal for human life and death; but his only true followers are Jews. They are the ones who live and die like him. If the Church has traditionally thought of itself as the true Israel, Wiesel, . . . seems to believe that the Jews are the true Christians. And, ironically, the Christians in their works behave like the Jews as the Gospels portray them. . . .

SHATTERING THE MYTHS

Can it be that Christian imagery is the most compelling way of understanding the suffering of the Jews? Can it be that Christian symbols and mythology, those of the faith system of the perpetrators of the Holocaust, suggest the highest ideal of behavior for human beings? Especially in light of the fate of Europe's Jews, would not the central Jewish ideal of *tikkun olam,* striving to perfect the world of men, be a more desirable goal for all men and, certainly, a more seemly one for Jews? . . .

Night is testimony that Wiesel's beliefs were shattered, at least for a time. Perhaps, too, Jewish symbols do seem to these artists inadequate or inappropriate for interpreting their experiences and those of the other Jews of Hitler's Europe. It may be that, in the eyes of Wiesel, . . . *tikkun olam* is an anachronism, and Christ-like death is the only possibility in a world which has been conquered by the Cross.

None of this, however, is the point of the [book], which does not really portray Jewish experience or Jewish belief. . . . For the most part, [it] attempts to interpret Christianity. [It] depicts the Christian world. [It is] heavily ironic and very biting. Wiesel . . . portrays a Holocaust kingdom in which Judaism cannot even begin to work at *tikkun olam,* its vision of a just and orderly society. Jews can only die. Their only decision is how to die. . . .

It is the nominal and the committed Christians, who prevent the achievement of the Jewish vision, and who do so, at least in part, by acting according to their own religious mythology and doctrine, supposedly suffused with love and mercy. . . .

In allowing the crucifixion of the Jews, however, Christians were destroying themselves as well. . . . "the sad-eyed angel" on the gallows, stands for both love and justice denied. [He is] Jesus as Christians have claimed to understand him. In the Holocaust, the followers of Jesus destroyed those Jews and, thus, their own central myth as well. . . .

There can be no question, of course, that the Christian imagery in [*Night*] . . . is intentional. It is too obvious to be otherwise. [Wiesel] . . . uses Christian symbols to interpret the Holocaust, viewing the destruction of the Jews as a modern version of the passion [of Jesus in Christianity]. . . .

[*Night*] asserts that the Holocaust was, at root, a Christian phenomenon and not a Jewish one, that foremost it raises theological questions for Christianity. . . . The Holocaust calls into question not the possibility of remaining Jewish, but rather, the possibility of remaining Christian.

How Wiesel Tells the Story That Can Never Be Told

Colin Davis

Elie Wiesel has often stated that the true story of the Holocaust can never be told. In *Night*, then, he struggles with the need to tell an impossible story. Colin Davis, the author of *Elie Wiesel's Secretive Texts*, suggests that the way Wiesel tried to overcome this dilemma was by utilizing very specific strategies. He wrote the story in the past tense, tightly organized his material, and by showing the reader how communication and language broke down in the camps, he prepared the reader to understand that "words will always fall short of truth."

Critics have implied that *Night* should be *read*, but not *interpreted*. [Holocaust scholars] Robert McAfee Brown and Ted Estess, for example, both preface their commentaries on *Night* with disarming remarks on the inappropriateness of critical analysis: "Of all Wiesel's works, [*Night*] is the one that most cries out not to be touched, interpreted, synthesized. It must be encountered at first hand." "One is reluctant to apply the usual conventions of literary analysis to the book, for by doing so one runs the risk of blunting the impact of its testimony by too quickly speaking of secondary matters. Against the horror of the story, literary considerations seem somehow beside the point."

Some readers have nevertheless insisted that *Night* should be read as a literary text. Denis Boak describes it as "a highly conscious literary artifact," and Zsuzsanna Ozsvath and Martha Satz argue that "the power of [*Night*] as a document of the Holocaust owes much of its intensity to its literary quality.". . .

RELYING ON LITERARY DEVICES

Night does not offer unmediated, uninterpreted realities. Events are filtered through the eyes of a narrator, Eliezer, whose primary function is to seize their meaning as he organizes them into a coherent narrative. He exhibits considerable control in his organization of material. The nine short chapters divide the text into manageable units that can be summarized as follows:

Chapter 1. In Sighet. Buildup to deportation.
Chapter 2. In train. Arrival in Birkenau.
Chapter 3. First experiences of Auschwitz. Transfer to Buna.
Chapter 4. Life in Buna. Hangings.
Chapter 5. Selections. Evacuation of camp.
Chapter 6. Evacuation through snow. Arrival in Gleiwitz.
Chapter 7. In train to Buchenwald.
Chapter 8. Death of father.
Chapter 9. Liberation of Buchenwald.

Throughout *Night* Wiesel uses the past historic tense as part of a retrospective narrative. He is "telling a story" in a way that becomes more problematic in his later, more formally sophisticated fiction, with its changing narrative voices, shifting time scales, and unstable tense systems. In *Night* the past historic gives the narrator retrospective command over his material. This allows him to organize and underline its significance, as well as to calculate and control its effect on the reader. Since this narrative mastery is important to the central tension of *Night*, it is worth briefly describing some of the means by which it is achieved.

Direct comment. The narrator interrupts his description of events and comments directly; for example, while life for the Jews in the ghetto is still relatively tolerable, the narrator shows the wisdom of hindsight:

It was neither the German nor the Jew who reigned over the ghetto: it was illusion.

Reader's knowledge of history. Much of *Night* is written in a terse, telegraphic style. Eliezer avoids commentary or explanation when the reader's knowledge of history can be expected to fill in gaps. The use of place names provides a clear example:

But we arrived at a station. Those who were near the windows told us the name of the station:
- Auschwitz.
No one had ever heard that name.

In front of us, those flames. In the air, that smell of burnt flesh.

It must have been midnight. We had arrived. At Birkenau.

Warning and premonition. The Jews of Sighet are constantly being warned of what will happen to them. Moché recounts the atrocities of the Nazis, but is not believed. In the train to Auschwitz Mme Schachter has a premonitory vision ("- A fire! I can see a fire! I can see a fire!"), but she is bound, gagged, and beaten up by the other Jews. Later, the Jews are told what will happen to them:

> Sons of dogs, do you understand nothing then? You're going to be burned! Burned to a cinder! Turned to ashes!

Eliezer's direct comments also have a premonitory function:

> From that moment everything happened with great speed. The chase toward death had begun.

Retrospective viewpoint. Related to the latter point is the way in which the narrator can explain what he did not know at the time of the events being described due to knowledge acquired in the period between experiencing and describing. He uses phrases like "Later we were to learn," "I learned later," "I learned after the war," "Many years later."

Repetition of themes. One of the central concerns of *Night* is Eliezer's relationship with his father and his ambiguous sense of guilt and liberation when his father dies. Eliezer's feeling that he has betrayed his father is reflected in other father-son relationships that he compulsively describes. Bela Katz, seconded to the *Sonder-Kommando,* places his own father's body into the furnace at Birkenau; the narrator refers to a child who beats his father; during the long march from Buna to Gleiwitz, Rabi Eliahou is left behind by his son, who has run on ahead, Eliezer believes, "in order to free himself from a burden that could reduce his own chances of survival"; and on the train to Buchenwald, a man murders his own father for the sake of a piece of bread.

Preparation of effects. Eliezer introduces striking or unexpected details that seem out of place at first, but that reinforce the impact of what comes later. After the first execution that he witnesses, Eliezer seems unmoved: "I remember that that evening I found the soup excellent . . ."; later, the cruel execution of a young boy is interpreted as reflecting the death of God, and Eliezer picks up his words from the previous page: "That evening, the soup had the taste of corpse." In Buna the treatment of the children seems to indicate a more humane attitude than we had been led to expect:

> Our convoy contained several children of ten, twelve years of age. The officer took an interest in them and ordered that some food be brought for them.

A page later, a more sinister explanation for the officer's interest is suggested as a new character is introduced:

> Our block leader was a German . . . Like the head of the camp, he liked children. Immediately after our arrival he had had some bread, soup and margarine brought for them (in reality, this affection was not disinterested: children here were the object, amongst homosexuals, of a real trade, as I was to learn later).

Through these devices, the narrator filters, interprets, and assimilates the experience of the Holocaust. Wiesel adopts a form and techniques that seem to confirm the Jewish expectation of the meaning of history and the interpretability of experience.

DENYING HIS OWN TRUTH

The essential problem of *Night* derives from the tension between the formal coherence and retrospective authority of the narrative, and the subject-matter of the work. Wiesel has always emphasized that the Holocaust can be neither understood nor described; it is a unique event without precedent, parallel, analogy, or meaning. This results in a problem of communication, and the survivors' predicament is particularly acute. They must, and cannot, recount the experience of the death camps: "Impossible to speak of it, impossible not to speak of it" (*A Jew*). *Night*, then, is written in the knowledge of its own inevitable failure: the survivor must tell his story, but will never communicate the truth of his experience; what is kept silent is more true than what is said, words distort and betray, the Holocaust cannot be understood or described, the constraints of reality ensure that the story will always fall short of truth. As Wiesel writes in *A Jew*, "In order to be realistic, the stories recounted less than the truth."

The failure of narration to command belief is reflected at the very beginning of *Night* in the incredulous reaction encountered by Moché the Beadle. Moché is disbelieved, his story dismissed as imagination or madness, utterly contrary to reality. Finally, he chooses silence rather than futile narrative. Later, Eliezer meets with a similar reaction when he goes to warn a friend of his father's about the liquidation of the ghetto: "- What are you talking about? . . . Have you gone mad?" Eliezer is reduced to silence: "My throat was dry and the words were choked there, paralysing my lips. I couldn't say another word to him"; and paradoxically it is this silence that convinces the father's friend: "Then he understood." In its opening pages the text describes an anxiety about its own status and its communicative capabilities. The messenger is unwelcome and his story disbelieved or dismissed. The narrative process itself is interrupted. Eliezer's father is recounting a story when he is called away to be told of the deportation of the Jews: "The good story that he was telling us would remain unfinished." The father's "good story" is unfinished and supplanted by the less pleasant story that the son will now recount.

The failure of narrative represented at the beginning of *Night* by these incidents is reflected in the writing of the text as a whole. The retrospective stance of the narrator and the control he exhibits over the presentation of his material put him in a privileged position of authority and understanding; at the same time, what he describes is the destruction of all points of certainty, resulting in the collapse of the interpretative authority that his stance as narrator seems to arrogate. *Night* is above all a narrative of loss; in the course of the text, family, community, religious certainty, paternal authority, and the narrator's identity are corroded or destroyed. The theme of loss also has consequences for the validity of the narrative. The narrator constantly expresses the desperate hope that what he is witnessing is not real; thereby he draws attention to the desire to deny the truth of his own experience, to subvert the credibility of his own narrative:

> Wasn't all that a nightmare? An unimaginable nightmare? . . . No, all that could not be true. A nightmare . . . It was surely a dream.

This does not mean that narrated events did not take place; but it does disclose a reluctance within the testimony itself to accept the validity of experience. While *Night* never discredits the authority of its narrator, significant aspects of the text seem to resist acknowledging what Eliezer nevertheless knows to be true. . . . The narrator of *Night* seeks to deny the evidence of his senses. The witness simultaneously suggests "this is true" and "this cannot be true."

WHEN WORDS FAIL

This tension is compounded by a mistrust of language, which, Wiesel has suggested, was corrupted by the Holocaust: "The absolute perversion of language dates from that period."

> If our language is corrupted it is because, at that time, language itself was denatured. Innocent and beautiful words designated the most abject crimes . . . The first crime committed by the Nazis was against language.

This corruption of language is reflected in the course of *Night*. The book begins in a world of confident speech: Moché the Beadle teaches Eliezer the mysteries of the Kabbalah; the father gives paternal advice; Eliezer narrates his childhood. However, the precariousness of this confidence in language is signaled by Moché's story of Nazi atrocities, which is true but discredited and disbelieved, and the father's never-finished anecdote. The rest of the text, and indeed all Wiesel's texts, fall under the shadow of these failed narratives. In Auschwitz language itself is devalued and stripped of its conventional meanings. Only one word retains its significance:

> The word "chimney" was not a word empty of sense here: it floated in the air, mixed with the smoke. It was perhaps the only word here that had a real meaning.

The degradation of language is shown most clearly in the use of direct speech in the course of *Night*. The advice and teaching of Eliezer's father and Moché are supplanted by the curt imperatives of the concentration camp guards: "Everyone get out! Leave everything in the wagon! Quickly!"; "-Men to the left! Women to the right!" The dialogue between Eliezer and his father acquires a surreal, futile quality as the son repeats the father's imperatives—now devoid of all imperative force—and begins to usurp his father's authority:

> - Don't let yourself be carried off by sleep, Eliezer. It is dangerous to fall asleep in the snow. You can fall asleep for good. Come, my little one, come. Get up.

Get up? How could I? How could I get out from this good covering? I heard the words of my father, but their meaning seemed empty to me, as if he had asked me to carry the whole hangar in my arms . . .

> - Come, my son, come . . .
> - Come, father, let us get back to the hangar . . .
> He did not reply. He was not looking at the dead.
> - Come, father. It's better over there . . .
> - There's nothing to fear, my little one. Sleep, you can sleep. I will stay awake.
> - First you, father. Sleep.
> He refused.

As *Night* unfolds the father's speech indicates most dramatically the decay of linguistic authority and the sources of traditional authority in general. Initially, the father is presented as a well-respected figure: "The Jewish community of Sighet held him in the highest consideration; he was often consulted on public affairs and even on private matters." In particular, his authority is reflected in his command of language:

> My father told anecdotes to them and explained his opinion on the situation. He was a good storyteller.

Eliezer first disregards his father's authority (he begins to study the Kabbalah despite his father's warnings), and then in his narrative, undermines the validity of his father's views. This is done gently in the early stages of the text; Eliezer's father sees little to worry about in the decree ordering Jews to wear the yellow star:

> - The yellow star? So what? You don't die of that . . .
> (Poor father! What did you die of, then?) . . .

As this loss of authority is taking place, the father's speech undergoes a decline from command to incoherence. His first speech in the book underlines his assurance and confidence with language:

> - You are too young for that. It's only when you are thirty, according to Maimonides, that you have the right to explore the perilous world of mysticism. First you must study the basic texts that you are capable of understanding.

This contrasts starkly with the unfinished sentences of his final speeches:

> - Eliezer . . . I must tell you where to find the gold and silver that I buried . . . In the cellar . . . You know . . . I'm wasting away . . . Why do you behave so badly toward me, my son . . . Water . . . My son, water . . . I'm wasting away . . . My guts . . .

The fundamental double bind at the core of Wiesel's writing lies in the fact that he must and cannot write about the Holocaust. His experiences during the war are at the source of his urge to narrate and to bear witness; at the same time, those experiences corrode the foundations of his narrative art as they undermine faith in mankind, God, self, and language. *Night* is a work sustained by its own impossibility: the need to tell the truth about something that entails a crisis of belief in truth. The tension of *Night* lies in its simultaneous assertion that what it narrates is true and that it cannot be true; such events cannot be perpetrated or seen or described. The narrator wants to believe he is mistaken at the very moment when he claims to be most brutally honest. So *Night,* despite its apparent simplicity, is a deeply paradoxical work: a first-person narrative that recounts the destruction of identity, a testimony in which the narrator wants most urgently to undermine his own credibility, a coherent account of the collapse of coherence, an attempt to describe what the author of the text insists cannot be described.

Wiesel's Literary Techniques

Mildred L. Culp

Author Mildred L. Culp analyzes the major literary techniques that Wiesel employs in writing *Night*. Rather than merely telling his story as a straight autobiographical memoir, Culp points out Wiesel's use of comic irony, narrative viewpoint, symbolism, and imagery. She believes it is the use of these techniques that allows *Night* to rise above straight autobiography and into the realm of art.

Night tells the compelling story of the Holocaust as only art can. It is at once historical and beyond history. A memorial to the dead, it is a living reminder of the need to reflect upon history for the insights it bequeathes the present. But it is told in the form of a story, which suggests to the reader that Wiesel values art for its ability to find ultimate meaning. To personalize that story, he juxtaposes the Holocaust with a child's recollection of his experiences and creates "a curious blend of beauty and suffering." The author's use of the first-person narrative makes his material even more immediate. This technique of memoir also transforms history into an organizing principle for form. The "I" organizes the form of *Night* and, finally, becomes its form.

Wiesel is in dialogue first with the "I" creating the memoir and then with the events of history that lead to a theology. The second dialogue proves more interesting than the first, but too many critics alight on it only briefly and bypass formal considerations. If Wiesel's "message" were intended to be expressed without the aid of metaphor, the author would have exchanged the memoir for an essay or for historical analysis. The autobiographical writing suggests that Wiesel believed his self-actualization could be communicated best through the medium of art. Therefore, it is formal

Excerpted from "Wiesel's Memoir and God Outside Auschwitz," by Mildred L. Culp, *Explorations in Ethnic Studies*, vol. 4, no. 1, January 1981. Reprinted by permission of the National Association for Ethnic Studies, Inc.

considerations to which we must turn.

Wiesel uses the tools of the consummate artist. Evidence of his technique appears throughout the narrative in comic incongruity, irony, temporal changes, symbolism, and imagery.

THE IRONY OF COMEDY

Comic scenes are created to magnify the tragic quality of the story. As if to underscore the seriousness of his subject, the writer refers to the wish of the Jews of Sighet that Passover end, "so that we should not have to play this comedy any longer." Passover, therefore, has turned into a religious celebration that is completely out of place. Later, after Eliezer is permitted to keep his pair of new mudcoated shoes, he thanks God for "having created mud in his infinite and wonderful universe." Under normal conditions, God is not usually exalted for the mud of the earth, and the universe of *Night* is not "wonderful."

In a world where comedy is incongruous, brutality transforms human beings. Just before the liberating Russian army arrives, for example, the prisoners dress in layers for the evacuation. Wiesel comments, "Poor mountebanks, wider than they were tall, more dead than alive; poor clowns, their ghostlike faces emerging from piles of prison clothes. Buffoons!" This scene is a reminder of the early incident in which the thinnest prisoner swims in his uniform, and the heaviest one is barely covered. But the reader does not laugh at this comedy, because the writer is recounting the life of suffering in a world where reasonable expectations are confounded and where human responsibility has been abandoned. The boy's world is dreamlike and must be shared through the story-telling impulse: "it was like a page torn from some story book."

If the reader misses the significance of the incongruity, Wiesel adopts irony as a stylistic device to communicate the irrationality of the concentration camp experience. The Jews of Sighet, crammed into a box car travelling to Auschwitz in the spring of 1944, have never heard the name of their destination. In fact, the group is so oblivious to its fate that it believes what it is told: "There was a labor camp. Conditions were good. Families would not be split up. . . . We gave thanks to God." The ultimate irony, thanking God at Auschwitz. Every sentence is clipped and matter-of-fact. Wiesel's genius is clear in his ability to keep the reader as aware of the deception in the "facts" as the Jews are taken in by them.

Irony strikes the reader once again on Yom Kippur, when the starving Jews debate whether they should fast. Some of the prisoners believe that challenging the danger inherent in observing the holiday under the circumstances of the concentration camp would impress God as devout. In this incident "the absurd [emerges as] the breakdown of the accustomed order in God's world, the dissolution of a long established relationship between man and God."

Hindsight Is 20-20

A third narrative device involves changing the shape of the dimension of time. *Night* itself denies temporality the character it usually assumes by repeating history and creating a perspective which shows the author within history and outside of it simultaneously. For the Jews, though, the present alone has meaning, because it is the abnormality, the very brutality of that present with which they must contend in order to survive. From this standpoint, the future and past lose their meaning. This is particularly noticeable in Eliezer's repeated comments about the inactive memories of the prisoners, and the reader's perception that the boy wonders only occasionally what happened to his mother and Tzipora, his little sister.

More particularly, however, the narrator leaps out of his story by presenting an analogous incident which occurred after the camp experience but reinforces its universal qualities. First the author establishes the dreamlike nature of the world by disclosing that Eliezer's senses are blurred when he arrives at Buchenwald. The transtemporal qualities of the Holocaust are disclosed in three specific incidents. The first occurs when Eliezer's father expresses minimal concern for having to wear the yellow star: "The yellow star? Oh, well, what of it? You don't die of it." Wiesel's aside, "(Poor Father! Of what then did you die?)" comes from the present but speaks of oppression against the Jews throughout history.

The second scene is Eliezer's beating by Idek. The child's blood runs and a French girl, who is passing as Aryan and does not speak with other prisoners, tries to comfort him. Although Eliezer is uncertain of the girl's background, the act reinforces his sense of her Jewishness. Wiesel then moves directly to his chance meeting with her on the Metro in Paris many years after the war. The significance of the meeting reflects that "the solidarity of Jewish people is based on the simplest and most courageous of human acts: the communication of one Jew to another that he is a Jew, and thus shares his identity." When the woman affirms their common heritage, the writer attests to the transtemporal dimension of the affirmation.

ART WAS *NOT* WIESEL'S GOAL

Author and book reviewer Robert Kanigel asserts in his book Vintage Reading *that Wiesel did not set out to create great literary art when he wrote* Night. *Rather, getting across the emotions of the young boy was what mattered.*

On the seventh day of Passover, the leaders of the Jewish community are arrested. "From that moment, everything happened very quickly. The race toward death had begun."

The race toward death had begun.

More artful writers might have avoided such language. Show, don't tell, says good writing practice. Don't destroy hard-won immediacy with flights of melodrama. This is not the only time Wiesel evinces such a superficial lack of literary polish.

Yet, peculiarly, what might otherwise be a defect here enhances the author's credibility. It is as if *Night* had been not so much "composed" as plucked whole from a ravaged heart. His is no mere pretty rendering, Wiesel seems to tell us. The horrors he experienced fall beyond the rules and restraints of "art." Giving vent to his grief, anger and despair comes first. He must throw in his lot with his town and his people, not with the worldwide community of literati.

Robert Kanigel, *Vintage Reading: From Plato to Bradbury.* Baltimore: Bancroft Press, 1998, p. 239.

A more arresting episode occurs during deportation as the Russian front closes. When a German workman throws a piece of bread into the wagon, a boy, like a ravenous wolf, kills his father over the food. And then he is killed by the other men.

But the author demonstrates that the significance of the incident is not isolated to the Holocaust, because he shifts to an experience in Aden some years later. In this particular scene some passengers on a pleasure boat are amused by the reactions of "natives," to whom they are throwing coins. When Wiesel sees two children on the verge of killing each other over some money, he asks a wealthy Parisienne to stop tossing coins overboard. She responds indifferently that she enjoys giving "to . . . charity." Each of these events illustrates Wiesel's perception that the experience and meaning behind the Holocaust are not confined to the concentration camp alone.

SYMBOLISM AND IMAGERY SPEAK VOLUMES

Wiesel's command of symbolism permeates his book. The symbols suggest death, evil, and insight. Each assumes a significance beyond itself and keys the reader into the main theme of the memoir, which is the opening of Eliezer's—and the reader's—eyes to God's dissociation from the events of Auschwitz. Indeed, the symbols in *Night* come to suggest that when humanity assumes responsibility for the Jews or any other group of people, God faces the death of God's creation and therefore moves outside of it.

Death imagery pervades the personal record, and symbols of life are transformed into symbols of death. Before leaving Sighet, for example, the townspeople are shadows whose lives are being drained. They are the goods of the market place, a commodity whose humanity is denied by the events of the Holocaust. In fact, the faded portraits symbolize the Jews of Sighet whose value has disappeared. Thereafter, the Jews are "dried-up trees, dried-up bodies, numbers, cattle or merchandise, rags, starved stomach[s]." Depersonalized and dehumanized, they are closest to death when, like the narrator's father struck down by dysentery, they become ghosts.

Even religious symbols hint of death. Altogether, these reflect the Jews' very real concern for their once vital faith. The world of Sighet becomes "an open tomb" leading to death. In such a place there are numerous travesties made upon Judaism. Hitler's agents choose the Sabbath to deport the Jews and the synagogue to detain them. This synagogue the deportees must profane by relieving themselves in it. Then at Birkenau, someone faced with the prospect of dying in the crematorium begins to recite the Kaddish. Wiesel observes poignantly, "I do not know if it has ever happened before, in the long history of the Jews, that people have recited the prayer for the dead for themselves."

Wiesel's imagery is most effective when it illuminates the omnipresence of evil through images and symbols of darkness and light. As in most literature, night stands for evil or death, but here light is distorted to mean the same. Fiery stars foreshadow the crematory ovens. Eliezer asks if his experience is not a nightmare and comes to realize that a series of nights, one "last night" after another, will introduce him to evil. Here he describes the first:

> Never shall I forget that night, the first night in camp, which has turned my life into one long night, seven times cursed and seven times sealed. Never shall I forget that smoke. Never shall I forget the little faces of the children, whose bodies I saw turned into wreaths of smoke beneath a silent blue sky. Never shall I forget those flames which consumed my faith forever. . . . Never shall I forget those moments which murdered my God and my soul and turned my dreams to dust . . . even if I am condemned to live as long as God Himself. Never.

This passage in *Night* incorporates many of the important images used by Wiesel and provides insight into his theology. It shows how the prisoners' days are converted into nights which darken their souls, but that God exists. It makes the light of the furnace satanic, because the furnace stands as a mockery of the candles lighted on the anniversary deaths of loved ones. In fact, the word "furnace" is meaningful as a reflection of the atrocity inflicted upon the Jews. As one theologian has observed, "A fire lit by men with the purpose of consuming men strikes at the very heart of creation," because this is a world overseen by humanity—not God.

THE WINDOWS OF THE SOUL

Eyes, Wiesel's most frequently used symbol, direct the reader to the Nazi *Weltanschauung*. In one moving scene, while a little boy called "a sad-eyed angel" is dying an agonizing death symbolic of the cosmic tragedy Wiesel recounts, the prisoners are forced to march in front of him and look directly into his eyes. Theologically, this is one of the must crucial sections of the memoir. Many readers have concluded that the incident symbolizes the death of God, when actually a close reading of *Night* suggests the slow destruction of a tortured child with refined and beautiful features as an act of humanity. When Eliezer says his own eyes are open to a world without God or humanity, he is speaking of Hitler's world. He remains above the bestiality of that world only through the act of reflecting upon it.

The concept of vision is abstracted by three prophets, Moche the Beadle and Madame Schachter, who are the seers capable of providing advance warning to the Jews, and Akiba Drumer, who appears to be a false prophet. The first two are victimized for their appearance of insanity. Moche is cast out; Madame Schachter, labeled insane. The mystic who has cabbalistic dreams of the deliverance of the Jews finds a verse in the Bible which may be interpreted to mean that his people will be saved within two weeks. Then the selection determines his fate. Wiesel's message is clear: medieval Jewish mysticism is irrelevant in the concentration camp, because the God of this tradition is not operative there.

Wiesel even enlists the aid of his reader's eyes when his characters may be unable to comprehend the significance of certain relationships. The orphaned Czech brothers who "lived, body and soul, for each other" are virtually inseparable. A rabbi and his son struggle to maintain eye contact. In particular, Eliezer's relationship with his father establishes a new covenant, and the two remain within the sight of each other whenever possible. All of these reflect the author's perception of "the crucial" importance of human relationships in the camps, which lend stability by affirming the importance of the human community in an inhumane world. They also show that God's covenant with God's people is still very much alive.

CHAPTER 3

Relationships

READINGS ON
NIGHT

The Holocaust Poisoned Eliezer's Relationships

Ted L. Estess

According to Ted L. Estess, author of the book *Elie Wiesel* and professor of religion and literature at the University of Houston, Eliezer's primary relationships were destroyed by the Holocaust. Estess claims that the relationships between Eliezer and God, the bond between him and his father, and his own understanding of himself were gradually destroyed by life in the concentration camp. Estess sees this as one of the most important points that Wiesel has to make, and believes it lays the foundation for Wiesel's later books.

Above all, [in *Night*] Wiesel is concerned with relationships. In speaking of the meaning of the Holocaust, he emphasizes this: "Something happened a generation ago, to the world, to man. Something happened to God. Certainly something happened to the relations between man and God, man and man, man and himself."

Night records how the Holocaust poisoned and nearly destroyed all primary relationships in Eliezer's life. His relationship to himself—and by this is meant his understanding of himself—is called into question on the first night at Auschwitz. He says:

> The student of the Talmud, the child I was, had been consumed in the flames. There remained only a shape that looked like me. A dark flame had entered into my soul and devoured it.

Eliezer's sense of himself as a pious Jewish youth jars with his situation in the death camp: nothing in his previous identity could prepare him for this confrontation with absolute evil. Faced with this discrepancy between his situation and his understanding of himself, Eliezer no longer knows who he is or what he has to do.

ELIEZER BEGINS TO LOSE GOD

His relationship to God is similarly disrupted. Immediately, Job-like, Eliezer begins to question the justice of God. How could God allow good people to suffer so? In accord with the pattern of reversals, Eliezer reverses the place of man and God. When, for example, the Jews assemble to pray on Rosh Hashanah, he comments: "This day I had ceased to plead. I was no longer capable of lamentation. On the contrary, I felt very strong. I was the accuser, God the accused." In much Jewish theology of suffering, God places the Jews on trial either as punishment for sin or as a way of further purifying the chosen people for their redemptive task. In *Night*, the relationship between God and man is first questioned and then reversed: God becomes the guilty one who has transgressed and who deserves to be on trial. God, not man, has broken His promises and betrayed His people.

While his relationships to himself and to God are crucial for Eliezer, his relationship to his father is important as well. Through much of his time in the death camps this relationship remains the single tie to his life in Sighet. Just as Eliezer's relationship with God is the center of the religious dimension of the story, his relationship with his father is the center of the psychological quandary. To Wiesel, the two relationships are intrinsically connected, but they are not reducible to each other. They are distinct, each with its own integrity and its own significance. Both add focus to Eliezer's identity, so that the loss of either is psychically disturbing, and the loss of both altogether devastating.

THE SON AND THE FATHER

The tenacity with which Eliezer clings to his father reflects an effort to draw back from the abyss that opens up with the loss of all human ties. The relationship functions as a touchstone to which Eliezer (and the entire narrative) returns again and again. He measures what is happening within himself in terms of what is happening in his relationship with his father. If he can sustain his unconditional commitment to his father, then something might abide in a world in which all is changing. Since anything can suddenly be taken away from the inmates of the death camps, Eliezer makes only one thing necessary to him: absolute fidelity to his father. God has broken His promises to His people; Eliezer, in contrast, determines ever more resolutely not to violate his covenant with his father.

Eliezer's struggle to maintain decency in his principal relationships finally focuses on this question: Will he betray his father and choose his own life at his father's expense? Eliezer watches one young man kill his father for a piece of bread; he sees another, Rabbi Eliahou's son, run off and leave his father in the snow. Gathering the last particles of outrage he possesses, Eliezer prays to a God whom he no longer trusts: "My God, Lord of the Universe, give me strength never to do what Rabbi Eliahou's son has done."

After the long journey to Buchenwald, Eliezer's complex relationship to his father reaches its culmination. Seeing that Eliezer's struggle to keep his father alive is depleting his meager energy, the head of the block counsels him:

> Listen to me, boy. Don't forget that you're in a concentration camp. Here, every man has to fight for himself and not think of anyone else. Even of his father. Here, there are no fathers, no brothers, no friends. Everyone lives and dies for himself alone.

In response, Eliezer reflects: "He was right, I thought in the most secret region of my heart, but I dared not admit it." Eliezer continues to struggle against what he considers to be the final debasement of his humanity: to choose himself over his father. But when his father dies, Eliezer makes this disturbing admission:

> And, in the depths of my being, in the recesses of my weakened conscience, could I have searched it, I might perhaps have found something like—free at last!

ELIEZER IS COMPLETELY ALONE

With this event the concentration camp has worked its horror completely in the boy's soul. In his view, he is guilty of having acquiesced in his father's death. The reader is likely to pity Eliezer, but Eliezer asks for no sympathy. In disclosing his feelings, Eliezer simply confesses the extent to which the Holocaust has corrupted the primary relationships of life. In stripping away a person's past, in pushing him to the limits of his physical endurance, in reversing all the expectations he had of man and God—in all these ways life in the camps forced the victim to choose himself without regard for the other. "At that moment,"

Eliezer sadly admits, "what did the others matter!". . .

An initial shock takes over Eliezer's soul when he sees that the Germans and his fellow Hungarians can be monstrous in their relationships to the Jews; a more unsettling disclosure is that God Himself can betray His people; but the final and perhaps most devastating shock arises from the disclosure that Eliezer himself is capable of disregard for his own father. The insight that no relationship is immune to the eruption of evil: this is what the experience of the Holocaust discloses to Wiesel. . . .

During his final months in the camps, the scope of Eliezer's world shrinks. He comments:

> I have nothing to say of my life during this period. It no longer mattered. After my father's death, nothing could touch me any more. . . . I had but one desire—to eat. I no longer thought of my father or of my mother.

Night reminds us that there are some simple and ordinary elements of human existence—food, trust, conversation, and, as a context for all things, human relationships—without which the spirit withers. Deprived of these things, the self can hardly expect to find significance in life.

Fathers and Sons

Ellen S. Fine

Ellen S. Fine, a professor at The City University of
New York and special adviser to the chairman of the
U.S. Holocaust Memorial Council, demonstrates how
for much of *Night* the strong bond between Eliezer
and his father (and other father-son pairs) is the
only thing that keeps them both alive in the concentration camp. Eventually the atrocities the pair were
forced to endure couldn't keep resentment and guilt
out of the relationship. Despite the son's ambivalent
feelings and thoughts of abandoning his dying
father, the Nazi's attempt to destroy the bonds
between them ultimately does not succeed.

If the nocturnal forces of death envelop and endure, miraculously, from within the depths of the Holocaust universe
surges the will to survive. Father and son struggle to remain
human, acting as lifelines for each other. They fight to keep
alive by mutual care and manage to create a strong bond between them in the most extreme of circumstances. Yet competition for survival causes a conflict between self-interest
and concern for the other. Close ties break down in the kingdom of Night and even the solidarity built up between
Eliezer and his father is undermined by feelings of anger
and ambivalence brought about by Nazi techniques specifically designed to destroy human relationships.

"A residue of humanism persists illogically enough in our
world, where there is a 'void' at the center of things," Wylie
Sypher observes, in *Loss of the Self in Modern Literature and
Art.* For a child of fifteen entering the perverse world of the
concentration camp, the "residue of humanism" is the presence of his father. Separated from his mother and three sisters upon their arrival at Birkenau, Eliezer becomes obsessed with the need to hold on tightly to his father's hand,
the only object of life in a universe where every moment

holds the possibility of death. "My hand shifted on my father's arm. I had one thought—not to lose him. Not to be left alone." Warned by an anonymous prisoner to lie about their ages, the fifteen-year-old boy and the fifty-year-old man instantly become eighteen and forty, and are thus able to follow Dr. Mengele's wand to the left-hand column (life) instead of the right-hand one (crematoria).

The fear of being torn apart from his last family link haunts the narrator throughout the book. During the "levelling" process, as he is being stripped bare of all possessions, he is fixated on one thought—to be with his father. Later, when the boy is recovering from a foot operation in the Buna hospital and finds out that the camp is about to be evacuated, he runs outside into the deep snow, a shoe in his hand because his foot is still swollen, and frantically searches for his father: "As for me, I was not thinking about death, but I did not want to be separated from my father. We had already suffered so much together; this was not the time to be separated." Upon arrival in Buchenwald after the long torturous convoy in the open wagons, Eliezer is again haunted by the familiar fear and fiercely clutches his father's hand.

This obsession to hold on to the father has been interpreted by the French scholar André Neher as juvenile. He feels that "Elie remains a small, dependent child in spite of the overabundant maturity resulting from his experience." However, if the gesture of grasping the hand is somewhat childlike, and the son's vow never to be severed from his father has a desperate tone, the primary relationship between father and son appears to be more an interdependency based upon mutual support in the midst of surrounding evil. Father and son, joined together in front of the sacrificial altar, recall the Biblical story of Abraham and Isaac (the *Akeda*), described by Wiesel in *Messengers of God* with the emphasis on commitment in a world threatened by destruction: "And the father and son remained united. Together they reached the top of the mountain; together they erected the altar; together they prepared the wood and the fire." Wiesel cites a text from the Midrash in which the Biblical pair are envisaged as "victims together," bound by their communal offering.

Until the last pages of *Night*, reciprocal devotion sustains both Eliezer and his father and is linked to the recurring Wieselean theme of rescue—saving the life of another human being and thereby saving one's own. The narrator reports several instances during which his father's presence stops him from dying. When Eliezer files past the fiery pits on the first hallucinatory night in Auschwitz, he has thoughts of suicide. He is deterred from killing himself by the voice of his father who tells him that humanity no longer cares about their fate, and that at this time in history everything is permitted. The father's voice, though sad and choked, represents a life force, which combats the all-encompassing blackness.

During the long march from Buna to Gleiwitz, the prisoners are forced to gallop through the snow, and Eliezer, pained by his throbbing foot, is again drawn to death as an escape from suffering. Once more the paternal presence helps him to resist the appeal of death. Because he feels that his father needs him, the son does not have the right to succumb. His will to survive is ultimately linked to the existence of his father:

> Death wrapped itself around me till I was stifled. It stuck to me. I felt that I could touch it. The idea of dying, of no longer being, began to fascinate me. Not to exist any longer. Not to feel the horrible pains in my foot. . . . My father's presence was the only thing that stopped me . . . I had no right to let myself die. What would he do without me? I was his only support.

After seventy kilometers of running, as morning approaches, the survivors are allowed to rest. The narrator sinks into the soft snow, but his father persuades him to go into the ruins of a nearby brick factory, since to sleep in the snow means to freeze to death. The open shed, too, is crusted with a thick cold carpet enticing its weary victims, and Eliezer awakes to the frozen hand of his father patting his cheeks. A voice "damp with tears and snow" advises the boy not to be overcome by sleep. Eliezer and his father decide to watch over each other: they exchange vows of protection, which bind them together in revolt against the death that is silently transforming their sleeping comrades into stiffened corpses.

Later on, when the men pile on top of each other in the barracks of Gleiwitz, Eliezer struggles to rid himself of an unknown assassin slowly suffocating him with the massiveness of his weight. When he finally liberates himself and swallows a mouthful of air, the boy's first words are to his father whose presence is acknowledged by the sound of his voice, "a distant voice, which seemed to come from another world." The voice once again is a lifeline, a reassurance against death. Yet the otherworldliness of the father's speech suggests that he is beginning to lose hold of his vital forces; eternal night beckons to him.

The last time the father rescues the son is in the open cattle car shuttling the victims from Gleiwitz to Buchenwald. On the third night of the trip, the narrator suddenly wakes up: somebody is trying to strangle him. He musters enough strength to cry out the one word synonymous with survival— "Father!" Too weak to throw off the attacker, his father calls upon Meir Katz, an old friend from his hometown, who frees Eliezer. The father thus saves his son's life through a surrogate, one of the most robust in the group, but one who dies before the men reach Buchenwald and whose abandoned corpse is left on the train.

During the various phases of the nocturnal journey the other side of the rescue motif is also apparent: the son carefully watches over his father and at times delivers the latter from death. These brief moments of solidarity disrupt the machinery of destruction and prove to be examples of human resistance in the face of the inhuman. When Eliezer's father is selected for the gas chamber in Gleiwitz, the youth runs after him, creating enough confusion to finally reunite father and son in the right-hand column, this time the column of life. Shortly after this episode, Eliezer saves his father's life in the convoy to Buchenwald. Lying inert in the train, his father is taken for dead by the men who are throwing out the corpses. Eliezer desperately slaps his father's nearly lifeless face in an attempt to revive him and succeeds in making him move his eyelids slightly, a vital sign that he is still alive. The men leave him alone.

Upon arrival at the camp, the father reaches the breaking point. He sinks to the ground, resigned to dying. Eliezer is filled with rage at his father's passivity, and realizes he must now take charge. "I found my father weeping like a child," he says when later he finds him stretched across his bunk, crying bitterly after being beaten by the other inmates for not properly taking care of his bodily needs. The boy feeds his helpless father and brings him water. We see here the reversal of roles: the transformation of the once-powerful paternal authority into a weak, fearful child and that of the dependent child into an adult. By assuming responsibility for the sick old man, the son becomes a kind of father figure, illustrating Wiesel's contention that in the inverted world of the concentration camp, old men metamorphosed into children and children into old men in one never-ending night.

The reversal of roles in *Night* has been viewed by André Neher as "an anti-*Akeda*: not a father leading his son to be sacrificed, but a son guiding, dragging, carrying to the altar an old man who no longer has the strength to continue." Wiesel's text, he observes, is "a re-writing of the *Akeda* under the opaque light of Auschwitz. It is no longer a narrative invented by the imagination of a poet or philosopher. It is the reality of Auschwitz." This reality offers a sharp contrast to the Biblical event. Whereas in the Bible God saves Isaac from being sacrificed by sending a ram to replace him, He does not intervene to save the father at the altar of Auschwitz. God allows the father to be consumed by Holocaust flames and the son is forced to recognize the inevitable—that he is impotent in the face of death's conquest and God's injustice. He must slowly watch his father acquiesce to death. Symbol of reason, strength, and humanity, the father finally collapses under the barbaric tactics of the Nazi oppressor to which Eliezer is a silent witness.

If the theme of father-son is characterized, in general, by the reciprocal support necessary for survival in extremity, the sanctity of the relationship is nevertheless violated by the camp conditions. In contrast to the son's need to protect and be protected by his father, there appears the opposing motif: the abandonment of the father. The Nazi technique of attempting to eradicate all family ties and creating a state of mind in which men view each other as enemies or strangers—what can be called the *concentration camp philosophy*—is demonstrated in *Night* through a series of incidents showing the competition for survival between fathers and sons.

Bela Katz, the son of a merchant from Eliezer's hometown and a member of the *Sonderkommando* [the squad of prisoners required to take the bodies out of the gas chambers and put them in the crematoria] in Birkenau, is forced to shove the body of his own father into the crematory oven. A *pipel* [young prisoners of about age thirteen granted power over the others in exchange for "favors" bestowed upon the S.S.] in Buna beats his father because his father does not make his bed properly. A third instance, and the one the narrator constantly uses as a measure of his own behavior, is the deterioration of relations between Rabbi Eliahou and his son. Shunted from camp to camp for three years, the boy and his father have always managed to stay together. But after the seventy-kilometer march from Buna to Gleiwitz they are separated. The Rabbi reaches the shed and looks for his son. He tells Eliezer that in the obscurity of the night his son did not notice him fall to the rear of the column. However, Eliezer remembers seeing the youth run past the staggering old man and is horrified by this clear example of abandonment:

> A terrible thought loomed up in my mind: he had wanted to get rid of his father! He had felt that his father was growing weak, he had believed that the end was near and had sought this separation in order to get rid of the burden, to free himself from an encumbrance which could lessen his own chances of survival.

Eliezer prays to God to give him the strength never to do what Rabbi Eliahou's son has done.

Perhaps the most devastating example of the breakdown of human bonds occurs in the cattle cars going to Buchenwald during the final phase of the journey. Some workers amuse themselves by throwing pieces of bread into the open wagons and watching the starved men kill each other for a crumb. Eliezer sees an old man about to eat a bit of bread he was lucky enough to snatch from the crowd. Just as he brings the bread to his mouth, someone throws himself on top of him and beats him up. The old man cries out: "Meir, Meir, my boy! Don't you recognize me? I'm your father . . . you're hurting me . . . you're killing your father! I've got some bread . . . for you too . . . for you too . . ." The son grabs the bread from his father's fist; the father collapses, murmurs something and then dies. As the son begins to devour the bread two men hurl themselves upon him and others join them. The young narrator is witness to the entire event: "When they withdrew, next to me were two corpses, side by side, the father and the son. I was fifteen years old."

Having witnessed fathers beaten, abandoned, and killed, the author, through his narrator, has chosen to represent the *son's betrayal of the father* and has omitted situations in which the father mistreats the son. As Terrence Des Pres has pointed out in *The Survivor,* the principle of jungle rule in the camps is frequently belied by examples of human solidarity. Wiesel elects to record the acts of care and decency performed by his father. By not being critical of the paternal figure in a world too often governed by viciousness, the author protects his father's image and honors his memory. This unconscious process of selection reveals the subjective aspect of the eyewitness account and of the survivor's perceptions. The focus upon the abuses of the sons is perhaps a projection of the author-narrator's own feeling of guilt; he identifies with them at the same time that he condemns them for having let their fathers perish. Despite Eliezer's efforts to save his father's life throughout the camp experience, the boy is critical of his own reprehensible behavior, and ultimately takes the blame for his father's death upon himself.

From the first day, the son helplessly witnesses the debasement of his father. When Eliezer's father is seized with colic and politely asks the *Kapo* where the lavatories are, he is dealt such a heavy blow that he crawls back to his place on all fours like an animal. Instead of defending his father's honor by striking the *Kapo*, Eliezer remains paralyzed, afraid to speak out. This fear makes him aware that his values are changing:

> I did not move. What had happened to me? My father had just been struck, before my very eyes, and I had not flickered an eyelid. I had looked on and said nothing. Yesterday, I should have sunk my nails into the criminal's flesh. Had I changed so much, then? So quickly? Now remorse began to gnaw at me. I thought only: I shall never forgive them for that.

This feeling of impotence is repeated in Buna when Idek, the *Kapo*, in a fit of madness beats Eliezer's father with an iron bar. The son's reaction is not simply that of a passive onlooker; he is furious at his father:

> I had watched the whole scene without moving. I kept quiet. In fact I was thinking of how to get farther away so that I would not be hit myself. What is more, any anger I felt at that moment was directed not against the Kapo, but against my father. I was angry with him, for not knowing how to avoid Idek's outbreak. That is what concentration camp life had made of me.

At the end of the narrative, when an SS guard strikes the sick father on the head with his bludgeon, Eliezer again looks on without moving, terrified of being beaten himself.

We see here the brutal effect of concentration camp life upon an individual psyche. Rage against the aggressor has been displaced onto the victim, and concern for the other has regressed into a preoccupation with self-survival, reduced to primitive and instinctual bodily needs. Eliezer is condemned to the role of the impotent witness, incapable of crying out, of seeking revenge, or, finally, of saving his father's life. Although he has fantasies of destroying his father's assassins, he can only behold his bloody face in despair. He is unable to respond to his father's last summons for help—an utterance of his name, "Eliezer."

Yet more than the sense of complicity, after the father dies the son feels ambivalent and even somewhat liberated. Earlier in the text, his mixed emotions surface during an alert in Buchenwald, when Eliezer, separated from his father, does not bother to look for him. The next day he sets out but with highly conflicting feelings:

> Don't let me find him! If only I could get rid of this dead weight, so that I could use all my strength to struggle for my own survival, and only worry about myself. Immediately I felt ashamed of myself, ashamed forever.

Eliezer's desire to rid himself of his oppressive burden, to lose his dependent father in the crowd, makes him recall with horror Rabbi Eliahou's son during the evacuation from Buna. When the narrator finally locates the feverish and trembling old man lying on a plank outside, he frantically claws his way through the crowd to get him some coffee. Later, he halfheartedly offers his dying father what is left of his own soup. While his deeds demonstrate care and devotion, his thoughts are of withdrawal and abandonment. Actions and intentionality, behavior and fantasies, do not correspond. The fifteen-year-old judges himself guilty: "No better than Rabbi Eliahou's son had I withstood the test."

The head of the block tells Eliezer that it is too late to save his old father and that instead he should be eating his father's ration. In his innermost recesses, Eliezer believes that the *Kapo* is right, but is torn by shame and runs to find more soup for his father. We see here the clashing principles for survival that dominated the death camp universe. On one hand, the rule of eat or be eaten, devour or be devoured prevailed. In the struggle of all against all, the *Kapo* teaches Eliezer, "every man has to fight for himself and not think of anyone else. Even of his father. Here, there are no fathers, no brothers, no friends. Everyone lives and dies for himself alone." And yet on the other hand, a *Kapo* tells the prisoners:

"We are all brothers, and we are all suffering the same fate. The same smoke floats above all our heads. Help one another. It is the only way to survive.". . .

The ambivalent feelings of the fifteen-year-old with regard to his father and food are intensified after his father dies:

> I did not weep, and it pained me that I could not weep. But I had no more tears. And in the depths of my being, in the recesses of my weakened conscience, could I have searched it, I might perhaps have found something like—free at last.

The relief soon turns into a deep sense of guilt, for having failed to save his father, for having survived in his place, and for having thoughts of being liberated by his death. The protector has been transformed into a betrayer. Unconsciously, the youth may even feel that he has acted out a son's worst Oedipal fear: he has psychically become "his father's murderer."

The survival guilt that Eliezer painfully endures culminates with the face in the mirror at the end of the narrative. Several days after the liberation of Buchenwald by American soldiers, and after a severe bout of food poisoning during which the boy almost dies, he looks at himself in the mirror for the first time since the ghetto. A stranger—a child of Night—peers at him, and the text concludes with the dark image of death itself: "From the depths of the mirror, a corpse gazed back at me. The look in his eyes, as they stared into mine, has never left me." The distinction made between *his* eyes and *mine,* conveying the notion of the fragmented self, is stressed in the original French: "Son regard dans mes yeux ne me quitte plus" ("His look in my eyes no longer leaves me"). The staring corpse is a permanent reminder of the "dead" self, that part of the narrator which was engulfed by the black smoke of Auschwitz and which will plague him for the rest of his life.

The cadaverous reflection in the mirror also suggests the son's identification with his dead father, to whom he remains attached. According to Robert Jay Lifton, survival guilt is related to "the process of identification—the survivor's tendency to incorporate within himself an image of the dead, and then to think, feel and act as he imagines they would." At the end of the night, Eliezer incorporates his father into his own psyche and projects this image onto the mirror as his double. The haunting specter with its penetrating glance serves to keep the paternal presence alive and is the son's means of defending himself against his loss. The mirror image epitomizes Eliezer's state of mourning and his desire to join his father, whose death is experienced as a death of the self. "When my father died, I died," Wiesel reveals. "That means that one 'I' in me died. . . . At least, something in me died."

CHAPTER 4

Literary Interpretation

READINGS ON
NIGHT

Night as Wiesel's Anti-Exodus

Lawrence S. Cunningham

The story of the Exodus from Egypt describes how three thousand years ago God led the Hebrews out of Egypt, fed them, and guided them to safety. Lawrence S. Cunningham, professor of religion at Florida State University, Tallahassee, and author of *The Sacred Quest* and *Christian Spirituality*, clearly illustrates that *Night* is the story of the "anti-Exodus." By comparing the focal points of both stories, he shows that the joys and victories of the Exodus mirror the horrors and death of the concentration camps. Cunningham believes Wiesel used this framework to tell his story to emphasize how the Jews felt abandoned by God.

The natural order of Wiesel's life was the God-intoxicated milieu of the Hungarian town of Sighet. This particular town was, like his own early life, insulated, timeless, unchanging. The events that began to unfold in 1943–1944 provided the immediate context out of which the natural order of Hungarian Judaism was changed and inverted into the death-dominated life of the camps. What has been largely overlooked is that Wiesel, writing some years after these events, frames the story of that inversion in terms of the oldest "biography" of his own people: the story of the Exodus. The life-giving biblical myth of election, liberation, covenant and promise becomes the vehicle for telling the story of the unnatural order of death-domination. It is as if Wiesel, either consciously or unconsciously, felt constrained to write a near parody of the Exodus story in order to give reality and urgency to the story that he feels is his vocation to tell and tell again.

The village of Sighet was a settled one. There was a rural rhythm, a sense of God's worship being done; a feeling of

Excerpted from "Elie Wiesel's Anti-Exodus," by Lawrence S. Cunningham, *America*, vol. 130, no. 16, April 27, 1974. Reprinted with permission from the author.

fraternity; and a longing for the Messiah. This village, as Wiesel remembers it and describes it, was a happy and secure place. An angel came to that village and told the people to pack up and flee, for death would come to them. The angel was Moshe the Beadle, a simple man who sought God in the mysteries of the cabala and who had seen, further to the west, the face of evil in the form of execution squads who shot Jews before open ditches. Unlike the angel of Passover, this messenger was thought to be crazy; nobody listened.

But Moshe had, in fact, been right. The orders came for the Jews to pack their possessions in haste and get ready to leave. There was a rumor among some that they would be sent to work in brick factories to the west. In this particular form of the Exodus, a people were to go out to make bricks as slaves, not to leave behind such an enforced work. But even that was to prove an optimistic rumor. The people left in haste, but they left in cattle cars for the west. During the train journey there was to be another mad visionary, Madame Schacter, who cried out to her fear-crazed companions: "Jews, listen to me! I can see a fire! There are huge flames! It is a furnace!" But she was insane, and her insanity was exacerbated by hunger, thirst, crowding and the stench of many humans in a small railroad car. Only when the train stopped at Birkenau, the reception depot for Auschwitz, did people look into the sky and see the guides that Madame Schacter had seen in her lunatic visions: a tall chimney that belched forth both smoke and flame. These flames did not, however, guide the chosen people. These flames signified something obscenely different: "Never shall I forget that smoke. Never shall I forget the little faces of the children, whose bodies I saw turned into wreaths of smoke beneath a silent blue sky. Never shall I forget those flames which consumed my faith forever."

A DIFFERENT KIND OF DESERT

When this new "going out" of the Jews was completed, the final destination was the desert. But it was not the biblical desert, where people wandered with a purpose. Here there was no manna sent from heaven to be found as the dew on plants in the morning. Nor was there to be a rain of quail to eat. In this desert the food that was sent "tasted of corpses." Nor was a brazen serpent fashioned and raised up in order for men to look on it and feel the venom of serpents disappear from their veins. In this desert there were other instruments erected and men were told to bare their heads and look on these new instruments: gallows in the courtyards where men were ordered to look up at children hung for camp infractions. And venom coursed through the hearts of the spectators to spew out in their thoughts: Where is God? Where is He? Where is God now?

That question becomes the central one for the inhabitants of the camps, and it is the central question of *Night.* The Jews of old were told to flee the fleshpots of Egypt in order to find God in the desert. They were His people just as He was their God. But in the new covenant of the anti-Exodus, people come into the desert not to be forged into a people, but to have their peoplehood exterminated. To be chosen in the camp meant to be chosen for the ovens. In an obscene use of the biblical vocabulary, election and "being chosen" meant to be marked for death.

Thus, the ancient dialogue between God and men now turned into a long and progressive silence in which the desert experience of Auschwitz and Buchenwald obscured and muted the presence of God. God became for the people of the desert someone to be accused and screamed at, not Someone who guided them into the wilderness in order to receive their prayer and their worship. The unfolding of this death becomes clearer in the novel if careful attention is paid to the parallel that Wiesel sets up between the death of his father and the death of his God. . . .

GOD NEVER SHOWED UP

When one studies the trajectory of Wiesel's relationship to his father in Auschwitz and Buchenwald, one is struck with the parallel trajectory of his fundamentally ambivalent relationship with the God of the Covenant, the God of Abraham, Isaac and Jacob. It is as though his own father was the icon of God. At the beginning of the experience in the camp, there was an unquestioned and unambivalent sense of the worship of God (Why do I pray? Why do I breathe!). The question of survival, an increasingly important question even to the point where it became *the* question, puts a strain on this intimate sense of obligation to God: to fast on Yom Kippur was to take a step closer to death since in the camp every day was a fast; to accuse oneself of fault on the Day of Atonement seemed to reverse the natural order of existence since it was the inmate who was grievously and unjustly offended. Slowly but inexorably there is a psychic transformation. One does not call for repentance or forgiveness, not even on Yom Kippur; especially not on that day. By some mad reversal that day becomes a special time to hurl an accusation. In short, to affirm the ancient covenant and its attendant responsibility is to hasten one's physical and psychical death. It is to hasten the day of "chosenness"—the day when Doctor Mengele will point his finger of election.

It is at this level that the whole drama of the Exodus becomes totally and completely reversed. The whole dynamic of the Exodus story is based on the idea of a people who must go out in order to worship their God in freedom and security. But the new Exodus ends in what Wiesel calls "the Kingdom of the Night." In the Bible God has found his people before they go to find Him. In the New Exodus, the people not only had found God but served Him; they went out only to lose Him. In the biblical experience the people are constituted and elected as a people by their fidelity to God. In this Exodus they are to find that their future means peoplelessness (forgive the neologism but how else can it be said?), framed in terms of a final solution.

In his recent work, *The Seduction of the Spirit*, Harvey Cox has emphasized the crucial importance of telling stories as a fundamental part of "being religious." Elie Wiesel has told his story within the subtle framework of an earlier story so that from this powerful mix of thanatography and liberation myth people may be forced to see the grim visage of postmodern man: the possible death of history; the dying of persons, peoples and comfortable divinities. God may not be dead for Elie Wiesel; there may be even a possibility of a new Exodus. Be that as it may, *Night* insists that the old order has been overturned and the form of the question has been radically changed. God may still live, but if He does, He has much to answer for.

Death Replaced Life as the Measure of Existence

Lawrence L. Langer

Out of the great body of Holocaust literature, Lawrence L. Langer, the Alumnae Chair Professor of English at Simmons College in Boston, claims that *Night* best shows the way that death became the measure of existence for the prisoners of the concentration camps. By focusing on this theme, Wiesel changes the consciousness of the reader so that they realize that life after the Holocaust can never be the same. Once Eliezer witnesses the murder of the innocent children, everything he thought he knew about life was proven wrong. As he watched people die all around him, he faced the realization that his life would now be measured only by the fact that he was not dead yet. The constant death chipped away at his soul—every time a prisoner died, a part of the others died with them. By the time of Eliezer's release, he was fully dead inside.

Most of the autobiographies concerned with the Holocaust numb the consciousness without enlarging it and providing it with a fresh or unique perception of the nature of reality, chiefly because the enormity of the atrocities they recount finally forces the reader to lose his orientation altogether and to feel as though he were wandering in a wilderness of evil totally divorced from any time and place he has ever known—a reality not latent in, but external to, his own experience. The most impressive exception to this general rule is a work that has already become a classic in our time, . . . Elie Wiesel's *Night*.

A reader confronted with this slim volume himself becomes an initiate into death, into the dark world of human

Excerpted from *The Holocaust and the Literary Imagination*, by Lawrence L. Langer. Copyright ©1975 by Yale University. Reprinted by permission of Yale University Press.

suffering and moral chaos we call the Holocaust; and by the end he is persuaded that he inhabits a kind of negative universe . . . a final rejection of love, of family, of the past, of order, of "normality.". . . Wiesel's *Night* is the terminus a quo for any investigation of the implications of the Holocaust, no matter what the terminus ad quem; on its final page a world lies dead at our feet, a world we have come to know as our own as well as Wiesel's, and whatever civilization may be rebuilt from its ruins, the silhouette of its visage will never look the same.

Night conveys in gradual detail the principle that . . . death has replaced life as the measure of our existence, and the vision of human potentiality nurtured by centuries of Christian and humanistic optimism has been so completely effaced by the events of the Holocaust that the future stretches gloomily down an endless vista into futility. The bleakness of the prospect sounds melodramatic but actually testifies to the reluctance of the human spirit to release the moorings that have lashed it to hope and to accept the consequences of total abandonment. Disappointed in a second coming, man has suffered a second going, a second fall and expulsion, not from grace this time but from humanity itself; and indeed, as we shall see in one of the most moving episodes in his harrowing book, Wiesel introduces a kind of second crucifixion, consecrating man not to immortality but to fruitless torture and ignominious death. Yet one is never permitted to forget what is being sacrificed, what price, unwillingly, the human creature has had to pay for the Holocaust, what heritage it has bequeathed to a humanity not yet fully aware of the terms of the will.

NIGHT VS. THE DIARY OF ANNE FRANK

Works like *Night* furnish illumination for this inheritance, an illumination all the more necessary (especially if one is to go on to explore the literature succeeding it) when we consider how unprepared the human mind is to confront the visions it reveals. . . .

Anne Frank's *Diary* was written in the innocence (and the "ignorance") of youth, but its conclusions form the point of departure for Wiesel's *Night* and most authors in the tradition of atrocity; indeed, their work constitutes a sequel to hers and ultimately challenges the principle that for her was both premise and epitaph—"In spite of everything, I still think people are good at heart"—a conception of character which dies hard, but dies pitilessly, in *Night* and in literature of atrocity in general. . . .

Yet Elie Wiesel recognized, as Anne Frank could not, that the values she celebrated might form an indispensable core for creating a magnetic field to attract fragments of atrocity, so that a permanent tension could be established between the two "forces"—a similar tension exists in some of the dreams we examined—a kind of polarity between memory and truth, nostalgia and a landscape of horror eerily highlighted by the pale reflection from vacant moral spaces. The literary effect is that memory ceases to offer consolation but itself becomes an affliction, intensifying the torment of the sufferer. Or rather, the usual content of memory is replaced by the harsh events of life in the concentration camp, until the past loses the hard edge of reality and the victim finds that both past and future, memory and hope—the "luxuries" of normal existence—are abruptly absorbed by an eternal and terrifying present, a present whose abnormality suddenly becomes routine. At this moment, life becomes too much for man and death assumes the throne in the human imagination. . . .

WHAT IS LEFT BEHIND

Night is an account of a young boy's divorce from life, a drama of recognition whose scenes record the impotence of the familiar in the face of modern atrocity; at its heart lies the profoundest symbolic confrontation of our century, the meeting of man and Auschwitz—and this confrontation in turn confirms the defeat of man's tragic potentiality in our time, and the triumph of death in its most nihilistic guise. The book begins with the familiar, a devout Jewish family whose faith supports their human aspirations and who find their greatest solace—and assurance—in the opportunity of approaching, through diligent study, the divine intentions implicit in reality. The premises behind these aspirations are clarified for the boy narrator by Moché the Beadle, a humble, sagelike man-of-all-work in the Hasidic synagogue in the Transylvanian town where the boy grows up:

> "Man raises himself toward God by the questions he asks Him. . . . That is the true dialogue. Man questions God and God answers. But we don't understand his answers. We can't understand them. Because they come from the depths of the soul, and they stay there until death. You will find the true answers . . . only within yourself."

With this counsel, says the narrator, "my initiation began"; but the kind of questions one asks in his dialogue with God are determined by tradition and education and assumptions that have withstood the assault of adversity. Moché's wisdom is tested when he is deported, together with other foreign Jews from the small Hungarian town. One day (having escaped, miraculously, from his captors), he reappears with tales of Jews digging their own graves and being slaughtered, "without passion, without haste," and of babies who were thrown into the air while "the machine gunners used them as targets." The joy was extinguished from his eyes as he told these tales, but no one believed him—including the young narrator. . . .

The citizens of Sighet, the narrator's town, depend on the material "items" of their civilization, almost as if they were sacred talismans, for security. Their abandoned possessions, after their deportation, become symbols of a vanished people, a forgotten and now useless culture.

Throughout *Night,* Wiesel displays a remarkable talent for investing the "items" of reality, and of the fantastic "irreality" that replaces it, with an animistic quality, and then setting both on a pathway leading to an identical destination: death. For example, in this description of a landscape without figures, crowded with things but devoid of life . . . in this passage, presided over by an indifferent nature, symbols of an exhausted past turn into harbingers of a ghastly future:

> The street was like a market place that had suddenly been abandoned. Everything could be found there: suitcases, portfolios, briefcases, knives, plates, bank-notes, papers, faded portraits. All those things that people had thought of taking with them, and which in the end they had left behind. They had lost all value.
>
> Everywhere rooms lay open. Doors and windows gaped onto the emptiness. Everything was free for anyone, belonging to nobody. It was simply a matter of helping oneself. An open tomb.
>
> A hot summer sun.

. . . The fifteen-year-old narrator of *Night* is gradually deprived of the props which have sustained him in his youth; but his experience is such that self-knowledge . . . becomes more of a burden than a consolation, and "a more valid conception of reality" sounds like a piece of impious rhetoric.

TRANSITION FROM LIFE TO DEATH

The displacement of life by death as a measure of existence is metaphorically reinforced in *Night*... by imagery that has become standard fare for much literature of atrocity, imagery facilitating the transition from one world to the other—the boxcars, for example, in which victims were transported:

> The doors were closed. We were caught in a trap, right up to our necks. The doors were nailed up; the way back was finally cut off. The world was a cattle wagon hermetically sealed.

"Liberation" from this hermetic world upon arrival in the camp, however, changes nothing; the "way back" ceases to have meaning, and man must turn his attention to absorbing the nature of the fearful "way ahead," and of finding methods to survive in spite of it, though the price he must pay for his survival is not calculable in figures inherited from the familiar past. He must somehow accommodate himself to an environment dominated by the macabre images of furnace and chimney, of flames in the night and smoke and reeking human flesh; and he must further acknowledge, against all his human impulses and religious training, the authenticity of this harsh, incredible fate:

> "Do you see that chimney over there? See it? Do you see those flames? (Yes, we did see the flames.) Over there—that's where you're going to be taken. That's your grave, over there. Haven't you realized it yet? You dumb bastards, don't you understand anything? You're going to be burned. Frizzled away. Turned into ashes."

The narrator's response introduces a tension that permeates the literature of atrocity: "Surely it was all a nightmare? An unimaginable nightmare?" With a desperate insistence he clings to a kind of emotional nostalgia, as if the stability of his being depends on an affirmative answer; but a subsequent experience shatters that stability permanently, and his efforts henceforth are devoted to making the reader relive the nightmare that continues to haunt him. His world crumbles ... over the suffering of little children: his first night in the camp he sees babies hurled into a huge ditch from which gigantic flames are leaping:

> I pinched my face. Was I still alive? Was I awake? I could not believe it. How could it be possible for them to burn people, children, and for the world to keep silent? No, none of this could be true. It was a nightmare. . . . Soon I should wake with a start, my heart pounding, and find myself back in the bedroom of my childhood, among my books. . . .

The waking dream, haunted by the omnipresence of death, filled with "truths" unacceptable to reason but vivid, nevertheless, in their unquestionable actuality, leads first to a disorientation—the new inmates of the camp begin reciting the Jewish prayer for the dead *for themselves*—then to an attempt, at least by the young narrator, to discover mental attitudes commensurate with what the mind initially finds incomprehensible. The ritual incantation which marks his inauguration into the concentration camp . . . it signifies not only a boy's despair, but the exhaustion of meaning in a world henceforth unlike anything men have ever encountered: . . .

> Never shall I forget that nocturnal silence which deprived me, for all eternity, of the desire to live. Never shall I forget those moments which murdered my God and my soul and turned my dreams to dust. Never shall I forget these things, even if I am condemned to live as long as God Himself. Never. . . .

When the first night ends, the narrator presumably has left normality behind, and death has infected his future: "The student of the Talmud, the child that I was, had been consumed in the flames. There remained only a shape that looked like me. A dark flame had entered into my soul and devoured it." The flame illuminates a vision of the self which under ordinary circumstances might be called self-knowledge, but here leads to a futility that negates tragedy and prefigures a complete exile . . . , a human condition that will have to create new terms for its existence, since Auschwitz has irrevocably breached any meaningful alliance between it and the past:

> Those absent no longer touched even the surface of our memories. We still spoke of them—"Who knows what may have become of them?"—but we had little concern for their fate. We were incapable of thinking of anything at all. Our senses were blunted; everything was blurred as in a fog. It was no longer possible to grasp anything. The instincts of self-preservation, of self-defense, of pride, had all deserted us. In one ultimate moment of lucidity it seemed to me that we were damned souls wandering in the half-world, souls condemned to wander through space till the generations of man came to an end, seeking their redemption, seeking oblivion—without hope of finding it. . . .

In the world of Wiesel's narrator, a diametrically opposite principle of negation prevails, whereby events silence the creative spirit, destroy the longings of youth, and cast over reality an all-embracing shadow of death.

Facing a New Reality

One of the dramatic pinnacles of *Night* illustrates this with unmitigated horror: . . . three prisoners, two men and a young boy, have been "convicted" of sabotage within the camp and are sentenced to be hanged before thousands of inmates. One imagines the boy, a "sad-eyed angel" on the gallows in the middle, the older victims on either side of him, a grotesque and painful parody—though literally true—of the original redemptive sufferer; the sentence is executed, and the prisoners are forced to march by the dangling bodies, face to face with their own potential fate. . . .

More than one boy's life and another boy's faith is extinguished here, and more than soup loses its familiar taste—a rationale for being, a sense of identification with the human species (as well as a divine inheritance), all the feelings which somehow define our world as a "civilized" place of habitation, are sacrificed on this gallows-crucifix, until it is no longer possible to establish a connection between one's intelligence and its apprehension of surrounding reality. The ritual of death, the agonizing struggle between living and dying which always has one inevitable outcome, even if some fortunate few should literally survive—for a time—the ritual of death ungraced by the possibility of resurrection, becomes the focus of existence and shrouds reality in an atmosphere of irrational, impenetrable gloom—"Our senses were blunted," as Wiesel wrote earlier; "everything was blurred as in a fog."

Under such circumstances men learn to adopt toward totally irrational events attitudes that one would expect only from insane or otherwise bewildered human beings: the result is that the incredible assumes some of the vestments of ordinary reality, while normality appears slightly off-center, recognizable, one might say, "north-northwest." Neither total confusion nor absolute comprehension, neither a mad world in which men behave sanely, nor a reasonable one in which human conduct seems deranged— this is the schizophrenic effect Wiesel achieves in his autobiographical narrative. It is scarcely necessary to arrange literal episodes or invent new ones to create the nightmare atmosphere which imaginative works in the tradition will strive for—such is the unique nature of reality in the concentration camp. . . .

For the victims who seek sustenance in their faith are reduced to a more degrading role by the subsequent episode,
a "selection"—which in plain language meant that some
men, usually those physically weaker, were periodically
designated for death in a ritual that resembled the weeding-
out of defective parts in a machine-assembly plant. Men
who know in advance that their life depends on the opinion
of an SS "doctor" run past this official, hoping that their
numbers will not be written down; most pass the "test," but
a few are aware that they "fail," that in two or three days they
will be taken to the "hospital" and never be seen again. After such knowledge, what humanity? What logic or reason
or connection between what men do and what they suffer,
can prevail in one's conception of the universe? In one's conception of one's self? For the narrator, existence is reduced
to an elemental struggle between acquiescence to death—
"Death wrapped itself around me till I was stifled. It stuck to
me. I felt that I could touch it. The idea of dying, of no longer
being, began to fascinate me."—and the need to live, in order to support his weakening father, broken in health and
spirit by the rigorous discipline of the camp.

DEAD INSIDE

Ultimately, the contest between Death and the Father, the
one representing the concentration camp with its insidious
and macabre dissolution of reasonable longings, the other
all those familiar inheritances which constitute the basis of
civilized existence—ultimately, this contest assumes symbolic dimensions, as if normalcy in its dying gasp makes
one final effort to assert its authority over the gruesome
power seeking to dispossess it. But when death intrudes on
the imagination to the point where memory and hope are
excluded—as happens in *Night*—then this rivalry, with the
accompanying gesture of resistance, proves futile; a kind of
inner momentum has already determined the necessary
triumph of death in a world disrupted beyond the capacity
of man to alter it. The extent of the disruption, and the
transformation in humanity wrought by it, is painfully illustrated by the cry of SS guards to the prisoners being
transported westward in open cattle-cars from Auschwitz
(because of the approaching Russian troops) to Buchenwald: "Throw out all the dead! All corpses outside!"—and

by the response of those still surviving: "The living rejoiced. There would be more room."

Thus disinherited, bereft of any value that might permit him to confront the inevitable death of his father with at least the dignity of an illusion, and compelled in the depths of his heart to accept the desolate rule of the concentration camp—"Here there are no fathers, no brothers, no friends. Everyone lives and dies for himself alone."—the narrator helplessly watches his last living link with the familiar world of the past expire and learns that grief has expired with him. Not only have normal feelings lapsed—plunging us into a shadowy realm where men cease to respond to reality by following any predictable pattern—but they have been replaced by attitudes which a "normally" disposed reader, still bound by the moral premises of pre-Holocaust experience, would characterize as verging on the inhuman. But to the reader who has himself submitted imaginatively to the hallucination-become-fact of this experience, the narrator's reaction to his father's death can more accurately be described as one illustration of what happens when human character is pressed beyond the limits of the human: "in the recesses of my weakened conscience, could I have searched it, I might perhaps have found something like—free at last!" . . .

At this moment, . . . the son . . . is severed from his patrimony and thrust forth onto a stage which requires the drama of existence to continue, though without a script, *sans* director, the plot consisting of a single unanswerable question: How shall I enact my survival in a world I know to be darkened by the shadow of irrational death, before an audience anticipating a performance that will be illuminated by the light of reason and the glow of the future? Out of some such query as this, representing a paradox of private existence, is born a principle of schizophrenic art, the art of atrocity.

The final, haunting moment of *Night* occurs when the narrator, Wiesel himself, following his liberation, gazes at his own visage after lingering between life and death (a result of food poisoning):

> One day I was able to get up, after gathering all my strength.
> I wanted to see myself in the mirror hanging on the opposite
> wall. I had not seen myself since the ghetto.
>   From the depths of the mirror, a corpse gazed back at me.

The look in his eyes, as they stared into mine, has never left me.

An unrecognizable face from the past and a living death-mask—variations on this confrontation, spanning two worlds with a current linking regret to despair, characterizes the literature that grew out of the nightmare of history which transformed a fifteen-year-old boy into a breathing corpse.

Night Is the Anti–"Coming of Age" Story

David L. Vanderwerken

Author David L. Vanderwerken contends that *Night* is the opposite of the traditional coming of age story. Instead of leaving the confusion of childhood for the understanding of adulthood, Eliezer travels in the opposite direction. His imprisonment forces his life to shrink and contract instead of growing and expanding. The adults that would normally be guiding his entrance into maturity are forced by their circumstances to abandon their roles, leaving Eliezer empty and fractured instead of complete.

One of our most familiar fictional forms is the story of a young person's initiation into adulthood. That the form remains rich, inexhaustible, and compelling can be confirmed by pointing to the success of John Irving's *The World According to Garp*, for one. Although specifically coined to describe a certain tradition of German novel deriving from Goethe's *Wilhelm Meister*, *"Bildungsroman"*—while untranslatable into English—has become our flexible label for hundreds of works that treat a youth's apprenticeship to life. . . .

Many *Bildungsromane*, especially modernist ones, gain power and point by parodying or even inverting the traditional formulae of the genre. . . . No better example of the *Bildungsroman* turned inside out and upside down exists than the story of Eliezer Wiesel in *Night*. In his chapter "The Dominion of Death" in *The Holocaust and the Literary Imagination*, Lawrence L. Langer posits that inversion, reversal, and negation are the overt strategies of much Holocaust memoir writing, skewed *Bildungsromane*, of which *Night* is the most powerful.

Traditionally, the story of maturation takes a youth through a series of educational experiences, some through

Excerpted from "Wiesel's *Night* as Anti-Bildungsroman," by David L. Vanderwerken, *Yiddish*, vol. 7, no. 4, 1990. Reprinted by permission of *Yiddish*.

books and classrooms, but most not, and exposes the youth to a series of possible mentors and guides who become, as Ralph Ellison puts it in *Invisible Man*, "trustee[s] of consciousness." Of course, Ellison's young man has trouble distinguishing the truth-telling mentors from the liars. Usually, however, such life teachers shape the youth toward a cultural ideal of adulthood. The function of education, mythologist Joseph Campbell tells us in *Myths to Live By*, is to shift the "response systems of adolescents from dependency to responsibility." . . . Often the initiation process is worked out on a journey, some movement through space, which has the effect of accelerating the rate of maturation. . . . And often the journey implies a spiritual quest. The result is a story of moral, emotional, intellectual, and spiritual growth. Normally, the initiate not only achieves self-definition, but also social definition, ready to assume a role in a community. . . . In *Night*, Elie Wiesel inverts and reverses, even shatters, the elements of the traditional paradigm.

TURNING OFF THE LIGHT

The very title itself implies a reversal since the *Bildungsroman* usually opens out into day, illumination, awareness, life. Instead, *Night* leads us into darkness and death. While the traditional raw initiate grows out into a knowledge of the richness, fullness, complexity, and multivariety of life—its open-ended possibilities—*Night* starts out with a sense of richness in heritage and culture that is violently and quickly stripped away, denuded, impoverished. Instead of expanding and ripening, young Eliezer's life narrows, withers, contracts, reduces to enclosure. Instead of finding a self and a place in the world, Eliezer begins with a sense of self, located in a coherent, unified community, and ends up when Buchenwald is liberated alone, isolated, and numb. Instead of becoming aware of his own potential, in touch with resources he was hitherto oblivious of in himself, Eliezer looks in the mirror on the last page and sees a corpse. The pious young boy of Sighet has been incinerated. And the corollary spiritual quest that usually leads to some satisfying accommodation or resolution . . . leads in *Night* to the void. Instead of climbing the mountain, Eliezer spirals into hell. And at the bottom lurk only questions, no answers.

The opening chapter introduces us to this pious and spiritual adolescent who lives in the eternal world, who knows more about what happened 5000 years ago than what is occurring in Hungary in 1943. The only son in a family of five, Eliezer has been groomed for a life of study, his future as a Talmudic scholar or rabbi tacitly understood. Now twelve, Eliezer feels impatient to delve into the mystical realm of Judaism, the Cabbala, if he can find a teacher. Although his father refuses Eliezer's request to study Cabbala on the grounds of his youth, precocious or no, Eliezer finds a master in Moche the Beadle, the synagogue handyman. In Moche, Wiesel offers an apparently traditional mentor character, the sage who will guide the initiate through the gates of truth: "It was with him that my initiation began." Moche is a Socratic sort of teacher, asking challenging and paradoxical questions that have no easy answers, if any at all. He tells Eliezer that the answers to all our ultimate questions are within ourselves. As a result of their studies, Eliezer says, "a conviction grew in me that Moche the Beadle would draw me with him into eternity." Suddenly Moche vanishes, deported in a cattle car with other foreign Jews, presumably to a work camp.

Just as suddenly, months later, Moche reappears in Sighet having escaped from the Gestapo, and he no longer talks of "God or the Cabbala, but only of what he had seen." Wiesel now reveals Moche's significance as Eliezer's mentor, neither as tutor of the verities of the ancient sacred texts, nor as agent of Eliezer's developing self-knowledge, but as witness and prophet of the reality of the Holocaust, a reality Sighet is not only oblivious of, but also refuses to believe. Consciousness simply reneges at Moche's preposterous tales of mass murder. The town dismisses him as mad; in Wiesel's withering refrain, "life returned to normal." Although Eliezer continues to pursue the truth of the eternal as Moche-I had taught him, it is the truth of temporal fact taught by the Lazarus-like Moche-II—his insights into the concentration camp, the kingdom of night—that will prove to be the most imperative, the most influential, perhaps the most authentic in Eliezer's near future.

WHERE HAVE ALL THE GOOD MENTORS GONE?

That, for Wiesel, only the mad could imagine the mad truth finds reinforcement in the figure of Madame Schächter on the train to Auschwitz. In chapter two, her hysterical shrieks of furnaces and flames are received like Moche's stories, an obvious consequence of madness. After all, she has been separated from her family. Finally, some of the people beat her into silence. Yet as the train nears its destination, she rouses to scream again, "'Jews, look! Look through the window! Flames! Look!'" Eliezer does look and realizes that Madame Schächter's cries all along have been premonitions, not psychotic hallucinations, for now he sees the chimneys of what he will learn are the crematoria. This woman of fifty becomes an indirect mentor who provides Eliezer with another insight into contemporary truth.

Of the other adults that Eliezer encounters in the camps, two stand out in offering contradictory advice on how to survive in hell. The first, the prisoner in charge of Eliezer's block upon arrival, makes a speech to the new arrivals that echoes the sentiments of innumerable, traditional moral sages:

> "Have faith in life. Above all else, have faith. Drive out despair, and you will keep death away from yourselves. Hell is not for eternity. And now, a prayer—or rather, a piece of advice: let there be comradeship among you. We are all brothers, and we are all suffering the same fate. The same smoke floats over all our heads. Help one another. It is the only way to survive."

Comforted by this plea for faith, community, interdependence, civilization, Eliezer thinks: "The first human words." Yet are they the "'teachings of our sages'?" For this condition? In Buchenwald two years later, after the death march evacuation of Buna, Eliezer hears another sort of advice from a block leader, at a time when Schlomo Wiesel is dying. This sage counsels Eliezer to look out for number one:

> "Here, there are no fathers, no brothers, no friends. Everyone lives and dies for himself alone. I'll give you a sound piece of advice—don't give your ration of bread and soup to your old father. There's nothing you can do for him. And you're killing yourself. Instead, you ought to be having his ration."

Of course, this is practical wisdom as Eliezer knows, but "I dared not admit it." Yet this is the ethical dictum of hell, into which Eliezer has been fully initiated. No ties are sacred.

Night's most powerful dramatization of an inverted mentor-initiate relationship is that of father and son. Schlomo Wiesel, respected community leader upon whom others rely for guidance and strength, represents the patriarchal Jewish father, a *mensch*, or as Bellow's Moses Herzog puts it, "a father, a sacred being, a king." Normally, the father helps the son make the transition in adolescence from dependence to independence. In the kingdom of night, however, the roles completely reverse; the son becomes the parent. In the end, the man whom others looked to has "become like a child, weak, timid, vulnerable." This reversal of the normal order is prefigured at Birkenau when the veteran prisoner urges father and son to declare their ages to be forty and eighteen, not their actual fifty and fifteen, the better to survive Dr. Mengele's selection. Indeed time itself does warp, becoming nightmare time, accelerating human changes. "How he had changed! His eyes had grown dim," comments Eliezer about his father the first night at Birkenau. As time unfolds, Eliezer takes the ascendancy in the father-son relationship, making decisions, taking charge of their common welfare, even feeling angry at his father for not knowing how to avoid the Kapo's wrath and getting beaten: "That is what concentration camp life had made of me." Although he never abandons his father the way Rabbi Eliahou's son had, Eliezer has his mental moments of filial disloyalty and betrayal. When they are temporarily separated during an air alert at Buchenwald, Eliezer thinks "'Don't let me find him! If only I could get rid of this dead weight'," but he immediately feels ashamed. However, when his father is carried away to the crematory in the night, perhaps still alive, Eliezer must face the terrible truth: "And, in the depths of my being, in the recesses of my weakened conscience, could I have searched it, I might perhaps have found something like—free at last." He sees himself, then, as finally no better than Rabbi Eliahou's son.

A Soul Emptied

Just as Wiesel radically overturns the stock *Bildungsroman* pattern of master and apprentice, he alters the traditional process of the evolving self on its way to fulfillment. On the day of deportation, Eliezer looks back at his home where he had spent so many years "imagining what my life would be like." The ancient story of youth's departure from the nest, encountering the world and fleshing out the skeletal self, becomes for Eliezer a story of decomposing flesh, of becoming a skeleton. Literally overnight, Eliezer tells us, his sense of self evaporated: "The student of the Talmud, the child that I was, had been consumed in the flames. There remained only a shape that looked like me." Even the name for the "shape that looked like me" dissolves with the engraving of

A-7713 on his left arm. The identity nurtured for twelve years collapses in one day.

Eliezer's sense of self is identical with his spiritual life. The worst of *Night*'s outrages, movingly worded by François Mauriac in the Foreword, is the "death of God in the soul of a child who suddenly discovers absolute evil." Again, the flames of the first night, fueled by the truckload of babies, "consumed my faith forever," "murdered my God and my soul and turned my dreams to dust." The two most powerful dramatizations of the consequences of Eliezer's sundered faith—the faith that had given richness and depth to his living—are the hanging of the boy and the first High Holy Days spent in Buna. For Eliezer, God is "hanging here on this gallows." If God is not dead, then he deserves man's contempt, Eliezer feels. The bitterness pours forth during Rosh Hashanah and Yom Kippur with the mockery of the prisoners carrying out the forms, the absurdity of the starving debating whether to fast. While thousands pray, Eliezer offers up outraged accusations:

> "But these men here, whom You have betrayed, whom You have allowed to be tortured, butchered, gassed, burned, what do they do? They pray before You! They praise Your name!"

Like Huck Finn, Eliezer knows you can't pray a lie:

> My eyes were open and I was alone—terribly alone in a world without God and without man. Without love or mercy. I had ceased to be anything but ashes, yet I felt myself to be stronger than the Almighty, to whom my life had been tied for so long. I stood amid that praying congregation, observing it like a stranger.

Also in this scene of the praying ten thousand, one can see Wiesel's ironic presentation of the community that the prepared initiate is to take his place in upon completion of apprenticeship, the culmination of *Bildungsromane,* public and ceremonial like the ordination of clergy or the commissioning of officers. This is a congregation of the living dead, a community of corpses acting out a charade. This is as anti as a *Bildungsroman* can get.

CHAPTER 5

The Legacy of *Night*

READINGS ON
NIGHT

Night Defines Holocaust Autobiography

Joseph Sungolowsky

As part of a collection of articles about the Holocaust in art and literature, Joseph Sungolowsky, professor of French literature and Jewish studies at Queen's College, focuses on *Night* as a defining work of Holocaust autobiography. He first discusses the elements that characterize a pure autobiography and then considers the difficulties and challenges that the writer encounters when the autobiography takes place during the Holocaust.

Autobiography is usually defined as a retrospective narrative written about one's life, in the first person and in prose. Such writing has appeared with increasing frequency in Western literature since the beginning of the nineteenth century. As a result of the events of World War II, it gained considerable significance. . . .

The history of the destruction of European Jewry by the Nazis has relied heavily upon the accounts written by survivors, which will probably remain a prime source of information concerning the magnitude of the catastrophe. Autobiography written as a result of experiences lived during the Holocaust is therefore an integral part of its literature. Since such literature cannot be linked to any of the norms of literary art, it has been termed a literature of "atrocity" or "decomposition." Holocaust autobiography inherits, therefore, the problematic aspect of both autobiography and the literature of the Holocaust. . . .

Autobiography is generally written in midlife by an author who has achieved fame thanks to previous works which have been recognized for their value, or by an individual who has played a significant role in public life. . . .

Excerpted from "Holocaust and Autobiography: Wiesel, Friedlander, Pisar," by Joseph Sungolowsky, in *Reflections of the Holocaust in Art and Literature*, edited by Randolph L. Braham. Copyright ©1990 by Randolph L. Braham. Reprinted with permission from the Institute for Holocaust Studies.

Writing autobiography at an earlier age or as a first book is considered an exception. Elie Wiesel's *Night* is such an exception. He recounts how fortuitous his career as a writer was in its beginnings, especially considering that he might not have survived the concentration camps at all. Upon his liberation, he vowed not to speak of his experience for at least ten years. It was the French novelist François Mauriac who persuaded him to tell his story, and Wiesel adds that at the time Mauriac was as well-known as he was obscure. Thus, at the age of 28, Wiesel published his autobiographical narrative concerning his experience in the concentration camps, first in Yiddish under the title *Un die velt hot geshvigen,* subsequently in French under the title *La Nuit.* In 1976, Wiesel stated that *Night* could have remained his one and only book; indeed, when he began to write fiction, the French critic René Lalou wondered how Wiesel could have undertaken to write anything else after *Night.* Clearly, at the time Wiesel published *Night,* he lacked the fame as an author of previous works usually expected of an autobiography. . . .

IDENTIFYING AUTOBIOGRAPHY

An autobiography is deemed authentic when there is identity between the name of the author appearing on the title page and the narrator of the story. In *Night,* Wiesel relates that during a rollcall in Auschwitz, he heard a man crying out: "Who among you is Wiesel from Sighet?" He turned out to be a relative that had been deported from Antwerp. Subsequently, Wiesel is called by his first name "Eliezer" by that relative, by Juliek, a fellow-inmate, and by his father. . . .

Autobiography is considered genuine when the author states, either in the text itself or in connection with it, that his intent has indeed been autobiographical. [Literary critic Philippe] Lejeune calls such a statement an "autobiographical pact"—an agreement between author and reader according to which the reader is assured that he is reading the truth. . . .

Wiesel's autobiographical pact was established twenty years after the publication of *Night,* when he told an interviewer: "*Night,* my first narrative, was an autobiographical story, a kind of testimony of one witness speaking of his own life, his own death."

Autobiography is written in order to come to terms with oneself. Recapturing the past is, therefore, the most common preoccupation of the autobiographer. . . .

Autobiography is written as a testimony, especially when the author has lived a particular moment of history that must not be forgotten. Such was Elie Wiesel's intent when he wrote *Night*. For him, "Auschwitz was a unique phenomenon, a unique event, like the revelation at Sinai." Had it not been for the war, he would not have become a storyteller but would have written on philosophy, the Bible, and the Talmud. He recalls that as he looked at himself in the mirror after his liberation, he realized how much he had changed and decided that someone had to write about that change. Although he had vowed to remain silent for ten years, he had absorbed "the obsession to tell the tale." He states: "I knew that anyone who remained alive had to become a storyteller, a messenger, had to speak up."

Autobiography may also be written to educate. The autobiographer wishes his reader to learn from his experience. . . .

RISING TO THE CHALLENGE

No matter how sincere or truthful the autobiographer intends to be, he must face the technical and literary problems related to the writing. Such problems are even more acute in the case of Holocaust autobiography. Before they write autobiography, authors will make sure that a reasonable amount of time has elapsed between the events they wish to relate and the actual writing. Such "distanciation" ensures orderliness to the narrative. In the case of Holocaust autobiography, the waiting period is not only technical but also emotional. Elie Wiesel states that he feared being unable to live up to the past, "of saying the wrong things, of saying too much or too little." He therefore decided to wait ten years before writing. . . .

With the best faith or memory in the world, it is impossible to re-create in writing a reality long gone by. In this respect, Holocaust autobiographers are even more frustrated. They constantly suspect that whatever the form and content of their narrative, they have not succeeded in conveying the past adequately. Wiesel feels that, while *Night* is the center of his work, "what happened during that night . . . will not be revealed.". . . However, since they represent an attempt to recapture whatever is retained of the past, such memories, as fragmented as they may be, remain invaluable. As put by book critic Leon Wieseltier, they are "all the more illuminating, because memory is the consciousness of things and events that have not yet disappeared completely into knowledge."

No matter how truthful the autobiographer tries to be, he cannot avoid having recourse to fictional or literary devices. Indeed, autobiography is necessarily linked to related literary genres such as the novel, the theater, the diary, or the chronicle. Thus, despite Theodore W. Adorno's contention that it is barbaric to write literature after Auschwitz, the Holocaust writer or autobiographer must engage in a "writing experience" if he wishes to express himself.

The terse language of Wiesel's *Night* is occasionally broken by harrowing scenes such as that of Madame Shachter gone mad in the cattle car or by dialogues such as those that take place between himself and his erstwhile master Moshe-the-Beadle or with his dying father. Fantasy is present when he depicts his native Sighet as "an open tomb" after its Jews have been rounded up. He uses irony when he recalls that a fellow inmate has faith in Hitler because he has kept all his promises to the Jewish people. Images express the author's feelings. Gallows set up in the assembly place in preparation of a hanging appear to him as "three black crows," and the violin of a fellow inmate who has died after playing a Beethoven concerto lies beside him like "a strange overwhelming little corpse." The grotesque best portrays his fellow inmates, "Poor mountebanks, wider than they were tall, more dead than alive; poor clowns, their ghostlike faces emerging from piles of prison clothes! Buffoons!". . .

KEEPING IT REAL

While autobiography may choose to embrace a greater or smaller part of one's life, Holocaust autobiography will essentially deal with the period marked by the events of the Nazi genocide. Just as any autobiography related to a troubled historical period acquires an added significance, so does Holocaust autobiography exert a unique fascination upon the reader because of its central motive. . . .

Evocations of childhood are all the more dramatic as they abruptly came to an end. . . . What follows . . . are scenes of departures. When Wiesel's family must join the roundup of Jews in Sighet, he sees his father weeping for the first time. Looking at his little sister, Tzipora, he notices that "the bundle on her back was too heavy for her.". . .

As painful as it may be to both author and reader, these autobiographical writings attempt to come to grips with the hard reality of the concentrationary universe. If *Night* has become a classic, it is because it remains one of the most concise and factual eyewitness accounts of the horrors. Wiesel goes into such details as the early disbelief of the victims ("The yellow star? Oh! well, what of it?" says his own father), the anguish of those who have been marked by death by Mengele in the course of a selection and Wiesel's own joy at having escaped it, the careless trampling of inmates by their own comrades in the course of the agonizing death marches. . . .

The Importance of the Word "I"

In a conversation with his friend and fellow U.S. Holocaust Memorial Committee member Harry James Cargas, Wiesel explains that the word "I" takes on great importance in his autobiographical writing.

In every word that we pronounce or that we use or that we hear, we must find the ur-word, the original word, the primary word. I would try to find in that word the tone of Adam, when he used the word. When Adam said "I" and I say "I," what is the link between these two "I"s? And this is true of all the other words. If I could read, properly, a word, I could read the history of humankind. This is language, of course, if you trace it, on the highest level of communication and of memory. Language, after all, is a deed of memory. Every word therefore contains not only myself, having said it, but all the people who have said it before me.

Harry James Cargas, ed., *Telling the Tale: A Tribute to Elie Wiesel on the Occasion of His 65th Birthday*, Saint Louis, MO: Time Being Books, 1993, p. 104.

"Autobiography," writes [literary critic] Georges May, "is capable of absorbing the most diverse material, to assimilate it and to change it into autobiography." Inasmuch as Holocaust autobiography deals with the events of one of the greatest upheavals of the twentieth century and the most traumatic destruction of the Jewish people, it is natural that autobiographers reflect upon the impact of those events on their personality, on the destiny of the Jewish people and on the post-Holocaust world.

Confession is an essential ingredient of autobiography. Its degree of sincerity remains the sole prerogative of the autobiographer who can choose to shield himself behind his own writing. In Wiesel's *Night*, the frankness of his confession serves as a testimony to the extent of the dehumanization he has reached as a result of his concentration-camp life. While he has been separated forever from his mother and sister upon arrival in Auschwitz, he has managed to stay with his father. Both have miraculously escaped selection for death on several occasions. Yet, the survival instinct has overtaken him in the face of his dying father. When a guard tells him that in the camp "there are no fathers, no brothers, no friends," he thinks in his innermost heart that the guard is right but does not dare admit it. When he wakes up the next morning (less than four months before the Liberation) to find his father dead, he thinks "something like—free at last." Henceforth, Wiesel's life is devoid of meaning. *Night* concludes with the episode of the author looking at himself in the mirror. He writes: "a corpse gazed at me. The look in his eyes as they stared into mine has never left me." As indicated by Ellen Fine, the shift from the first to the third person in that sentence points to the "fragmented self," and, as indicated by Wiesel himself, that sight was to determine his career as a "writer-witness.". . .

So Others Will Understand

Meant as a stark narrative of the events and despite the ten-year period that preceded its writing, Wiesel's *Night* is devoid of reflections extraneous to his experiences in the concentration camps. He has stated that, except for *Night*, his other works are not autobiographical, although he occasionally brings into them "autobiographical data and moods." Yet, Wiesel has emphasized the importance of *Night as* the foundation of his subsequent works. He states: "*Night*, my first narrative, was an autobiographical story, a kind of testimony of one witness speaking of his own life, his own death. All kinds of options were available: suicide, madness, killing, political action, hate, friendship. I note all these options: faith, rejection of faith, blasphemy, atheism, denial, rejection of man, despair, and in each book I explore one aspect. In *Dawn*, I explore the political action; in *The Accident*, suicide; in *The Town Beyond the Wall*, madness; in *The Gates of the Forest*, faith and friendship; in *A Beggar in Jerusalem*, history, the return. All the stories are one story except that I build them in concentric circles. The center is the same and is in *Night*." Such a position illustrates Philippe Lejeune's concept of "autobiographical space." Indeed, according to Lejeune, it is not always possible to derive the total image of a writer solely on the basis of a work explicitly declared to be autobiographical. Such an image is to be sought rather in the totality of his work which cannot fail to contain autobiographical data. Reflections on Jewish destiny and identity and on the post-Holocaust world are surely the very essence of Wiesel's writings whether they take the form of fiction, tales, plays, or essays.

Autobiography does not necessarily encompass a whole life. Many autobiographers choose to write about a part of it which they deem significant enough to reflect a profound if not crucial human experience. The Holocaust illustrates this aspect of autobiographical writing. . . . [Holocaust autobiographers] feel a compelling need at one point or another in their lives to tell of their experiences. Whether they write to settle the past, to testify or to educate, they mobilize a variety of devices and themes available to the autobiographer who seeks to share his experiences with the reader. As the Holocaust continues to be represented in an ever-growing multiplicity of forms, autobiography remains a fascinating means to express it. It is noteworthy, therefore, that the Holocaust autobiographer encounters consciously or not many of the problems faced by any autobiographer. However, in the case of the Holocaust autobiographer, such problems become even more crucial because of the nature of the material he is dealing with. Autobiography universalizes one's life. In the hands of Wiesel, Holocaust autobiography not only serves as an invaluable testimony of events that must never be forgotten, but also strengthens the feeling of all those who wish to identify with the victims of the greatest crime that ever took place amidst modern civilization.

Why People Resist the Truth

Ora Avni

Ora Avni, a professor of French at Yale University and the author of an upcoming book on post-Holocaust historical consciousness, addresses the disbelief people exhibit when presented with Holocaust testimony. Before and during the Holocaust there were many cases where warnings went unheeded. It seemed that no one—not the European Jews nor the world at large—could believe such atrocities against humanity were actually happening. Avni suggests that one reason for this is that people need a framework, a background to draw from, before they can process new ideas. And before the Holocaust, no one could conceive of such evil. They resist making the truth part of their reality. He demonstrates how Wiesel took this knowledge and framed *Night* so that readers would be able to shed their own disbelief.

[*Night's*] opening focuses not so much on the boy, however, as on a foreigner, Moshe the Beadle, a wretched yet good-natured and lovable dreamer, versed in Jewish mysticism. When the town's foreign Jews are deported by the Nazis to an unknown destination, he leaves with them; but he comes back. Having miraculously survived the murder of his convoy, he hurries back to warn the others. No longer singing, humming, or praying, he plods from door to door, desperately repeating the same stories of calm and dispassionate killings. But, despite his unrelenting efforts, "people refused not only to believe his stories, but even to listen to them."

Like Moshe the Beadle, the first survivors who told their stories either to other Jews or to the world were usually met with disbelief. When the first escapees from Ponar's killing grounds tried to warn the Vilna ghetto that they were not

Excerpted from "Beyond Psychoanalysis: Elie Wiesel's *Night* in Historical Perspective," by Ora Avni, in *Auschwitz and After*, edited by Lawrence D. Kritzman (New York: Routledge, 1995). Reprinted by permission of Ora Avni.

sent to work but to be murdered, not only did the Jews not believe them, but they accused the survivors of demoralizing the ghetto, and demanded that they stop spreading such stories. Similarly, when Jan Karski, the courier of the Polish government-in-exile who had smuggled himself into the Warsaw Ghetto so that he could report the Nazi's atrocities as an eyewitness, made his report to Justice Felix Frankfurter, the latter simply said, "I don't believe you." Asked to explain, he added, "I did not say that this young man is lying. I said I cannot believe him. There is a difference." How are we to understand this disbelief? What are its causes and effects, and above all, what lesson can we learn from it? . . .

FROM THE BEGINNING

We must also note that Moshe the Beadle's narrative does not only *open* the boy's narrative as it first appears, but frames it on both ends: once the reader is aware of the consequences of telling such a story, he or she extends this awareness to the story told by the boy. The opening episode thus invites the reader to read beyond the abrupt end of *Night*, all the way to the moment absent from *Night* proper, when the newly freed boy tells his own tale of survival: will this story, too, meet with hostility, disbelief, and denial? (And who better than the reader knows that the boy did eventually tell his story, and that this tale constitutes the very text he or she is reading?) The scene of narration of the opening episode thus prefigures the scene of reading of *Night*. . . . It warns the reader of the consequences of disbelief no less than it warns the town folks.

Shoah [another word for the Holocaust] narratives have given rise to a host of false problems. Faced with the horror of the *Shoah* and the suffering of its survivors, some have felt overwhelmed and, overcome with a sense of simple human decency, have questioned their right to examine an extreme experience in which they had no part. These scruples are, I think, misplaced: no one questions the right, or even the need of survivors to sort out their experience, or to bear witness. We readily concede survivors' wish and right to bear witness, to leave a historical account of their ordeal for posterity. But what about this posterity (ourselves), what about the recipients of those narratives? We—the latecomers to the experience of the *Shoah*—shall never be able to fully grasp the abysmal suffering and despair of the survivors.

And yet, not only do we share with them a scene of narration, but our participation in this scene of narration may have become the organizing principle of our lives and our own historical imperative. How, then, are we going to face up to this task? Like the town folks, we have gone through disbelief and denial. But today, two generations later, we have rediscovered the *Shoah,* as the numerous publications on the subject will attest (some even claim that we have trivialized the *Shoah* with excessive verbiage). How, then, are we to dispose of the knowledge conveyed by survivors' narratives? How can we integrate the lesson of their testimonies in our historical project—at least, if ours is a project in which there is no room for racial discrimination, genocide, acquiescence to evil, passive participation in mass murder; a project in which "get involved" has come to replace "look the other way"? . . .

Like Moshe, Wiesel came back; like Moshe, he told his story; and like Moshe, he told it again and again. It is therefore not merely a question of informing others (for information purposes, once the story is told, one need not tell it again). Like Moshe, Wiesel clearly does not set out to impart information only, but to *tell the tale,* that is, to share a scene of narration with a community of readers. This explains why, while the *Shoah* is in fact the subject of all his texts, Wiesel, wiser than Moshe, never recounted his actual experience in the death camps again. Like the opening episode of *Night,* his other works deal with "before" and "after": before, as a premonition of things to come; after, as a call for latecomers to see themselves accountable for living in a post-*Shoah* world. The opening episode thus encapsulates Wiesel's life project, in that it invites us to reflect not only on the nature of the *Shoah* itself, but first, on living historically (that is, on living in a world of which the *Shoah* is part), and second, on transmitting this history from one person and one generation to the other. . . .

To what, then, does this episode owe its exemplary value? Why has Moshe, the ultimate *Shoah* survivor-narrator, come back? Why does he feel compelled to endlessly repeat his story? Why does he no longer pray? On the other hand, why are his listeners so recalcitrant? Why do they not believe him? Why do they accuse him of madness or of ulterior motives? Why do they all but gag him? That this episode illustrates widespread attitudes towards all accounts of Nazi

TRIAL RUN FOR NUCLEAR WAR?

A. Alvarez, essayist and renowned literary critic, declares in Beyond All This Fiddle *that decades after it ended, the Holocaust still haunts us because of what it could indicate for our future.*

The atrocities [of the Holocaust] have in no way been diminished by the passage of time, but their meaning has changed slightly, and in changing it has become more, rather than less, urgent. In the beginning, the horror of the camps was heightened by a certain relief—'Thank God it wasn't me'—and this in turn provoked guilt. To judge from their writing, even former inmates seem to have felt obscurely guilty at having survived when friends and family had gone under—as though survival were almost a mark of cowardice, as though it certainly meant, for them, that they had had to compromise with the omnipresent and contagious corruption. For the rest of us, there was the far obscurer guilt of being Jews who had never been exposed to the camps at all. In these circumstances, the rhetoric of so much concentration-camp literature was comforting; it enabled us to feel engaged while in reality preserving our safe distance. Since then the situation has changed. The question of survival is less obvious, but more ubiquitous, more pervasive. I once suggested (in a piece for *The Atlantic Monthly,* December 1962) that one of the reasons why the camps continue to keep such a tight hold on our imaginations is that we see in them a small-scale trial run for a nuclear war.

atrocities and Jewish victimization is unquestionable. We shall therefore focus on the *self-positioning* of the subject (teller or listener, knowledgeable or uninformed) in the face of accounts of the *Shoah,* be it at the dinner table, in the classroom, on the psychoanalyst's couch, in academe, or in the morning paper. . . .

LISTEN TO ME

The *Shoah* has shaken our vision of man so profoundly that, half a century later, we are still grappling with its aftermath, with our urgent albeit terrifying need for a radical reevaluation of our concept of man-in-the-world. And, as the reluctance to believe the stories or even to listen to them shows, this reevaluation does not befall only those who were the subjects of the event or their children (victims, perpetrators, or even bystanders). It extends to an entire generation. As

Between 1940 and 1945, four-and-a-half-million people died in Auschwitz; the same number would die in minutes if a hydrogen bomb landed on London or New York. Then there are those other curious, upside-down similarities: the use of modern industrial processes for the mass production of corpses, with all the attendant paraphernalia of efficiency, meticulous paperwork and bureaucratic organization; the deliberate annihilation not merely of lives but of identities, as in some paranoid vision of a mass culture. And so on. It adds up to a perverted, lunatic parody of our own engulfing but otherwise comfortable technological societies. So the literature of the camps has become, insidiously and unanswerably, our own under-literature. Its connections with our lives, our despairs, our fantasies are subterranean but constant and powerful. When the façade of our bright, jazzy, careless affluence rifts, and our well-conditioned domestic psyches explode, what oozes out is the same sour destructiveness—passive or active, the need to destroy or be destroyed—as once, for some years, contaminated almost the whole of European morality. If our century has invented unprecedented ways of making life easier, it has also provided us with multitudinous, sophisticated, and equally unprecedented means of annihilation. The camps are a proof of that, and a working model. In them the language of our sickness was created.

A. Alvarez, "The Literature of the Holocaust" in *Beyond All This Fiddle*, New York: Penguin Press, 1968, pp. 23–24.

[writer] Terence des Pres rightly notes, "the self's sense of itself is different now, and what has made the difference, both as cause and continuing condition, is simply knowing that the Holocaust occurred.". . .

The exemplary value of *Night*'s opening episode hinges upon its containing the narrative of Eliezer, and by extension of any survivor, within the problems raised by this self-positioning.

Prior to his own encounter with Nazism, he asks Moshe: "Why are you so anxious that people should believe what you say? In your place, I shouldn't care whether they believe me or not. . .". Indeed, in comparison with the ordeal from which he has just escaped, there seems to be little reason for Moshe's present distress. What, then, hangs upon the credibility of his story? Why do the town people refuse to listen to the beadle? What effect does their reaction have on the *pro-*

ject that brought him back to town? Somehow tentatively, Moshe answers the boy's query:

> "You don't understand," he said in despair. "You can't understand. I have been saved miraculously. I managed to get back here. Where did I get the strength from? I wanted to come back to Sighet to tell you the story of my death. So that you could prepare yourselves while there was still time. To live? I don't attach any importance to my life any more. I'm alone. No, I wanted to come back, and to warn you. And see how it is, no one will listen to me. . . ."

Moshe's anguished insistence on being heard undoubtedly illustrates the well-known recourse to narrative in order to impose coherence on an incoherent experience (a commonplace of literary criticism), to work through a trauma (a commonplace of psychoanalysis), the laudable drive to testify to a crime (a commonplace of *Shoah* narratives), or even the heroics of saving others (a commonplace of resistance literature). Although such readings of *Night* are certainly not irrelevant, I do not think that they do justice to the gripping urgency of his unwelcome and redundant narrative, unless we read the text literally: Moshe came back "to tell you the story."

We must rule out simply imparting knowledge, since Moshe's undertaking clearly does not stop at communicating the story. A scenario in which the town folks gather around him to listen to his story, and then go on about their business would be absurd. In this case, to "believe" the story is to be affected by it. Moshe's story is therefore a speech act. Allow me an example to clarify this last point: Paul Revere tearing through the countryside and screaming "The British are coming!" His message was immediately understood. No one suspected him of either madness or excessive need of attention. Unlike Moshe and the town folks, and unlike *Shoah* survivors and ourselves, Paul Revere and his New Englanders lived in the same world, a world in which British might and probably would come; a world in which that would be a very bad thing indeed; and a world in which should they come, clear measures must be taken. If the story is to realize its illocutionary force, not only does it have to be integrated into its listeners' stock of "facts they know about their world," but it must also rely on a known formula (a convention) by which an individual reacts to such knowledge. For example, one has to know that if the British are coming, one is expected to arm oneself and prepare for resistance (a clean shave would be a highly inappropriate reaction to Paul Revere's message). Revere could therefore speedily spread his message while never dismounting his horse, and still secure its uptake. In short, to be a felicitous speech act, the story must affect its listeners in an expected, conventional manner (that is, following clear precedents). Until it does, its force is void.

TOO BIG A BURDEN

Speech act theorists unanimously agree on the conventional aspect of a speech act, that is, on its reliance on a preexisting convention shared by the community of its listeners. But sometimes, such a precise convention does not exist. It has to be inferred and activated out of the stock of beliefs and conventions that both utterer and listeners find workable, plausible, and altogether acceptable. In invoking their shared beliefs, the felicitous speech act thus becomes a *rallying point* for the utterer and the listeners. It binds them together. A community is therefore as much the *result* of its speech acts as it is the necessary condition for their success. In other words, if, as he claims, Moshe came back to town in order to tell his story, and if indeed he is determined to secure the felicitous uptake of his narrative's illocutionary force, then this determination reveals yet *another project,* one that is even more exacting in that it affects his (and his fellow villagers') being-in-the-world: his return to town is also an attempt to reaffirm his ties to his community (its conventions, its values), to reintegrate into the human community of his past—a community whose integrity was put into question by the absurd, incomprehensible, and unassimilable killings he had witnessed. Through his encounter with Nazism, Moshe has witnessed not only the slaughter of a human cargo, but the demise of his notion of humanity— a notion, however, still shared by the town folks. As long as they hold on to this notion of humanity to which he can no longer adhere, he is, *ipso facto,* a freak. Coming back to town to tell his story to a receptive audience is therefore Moshe's way back to normalcy, back to humanity. Only by having a community integrate his dehumanizing experience into the narratives of self-representation that it shares and infer a new code of behavior based on the information he is imparting, only by becoming part of this community's history, can Moshe hope to reclaim his lost humanity (the question remains, as we shall see, at what price to that community). It is therefore not a question of privately telling the story as of having others—a whole community—*claim* it, *appropriate* it, and *react* (properly) to it.

The closing scene of *Night* echoes this concern. Upon his liberation by American troops, the narrator first rushes to a mirror to look at himself. Is he still himself? Can the mirror show him unchanged since the last time he looked at himself in the mirror, before he was taken out of his village? Can he reintegrate into himself? Will the mirror allow him to bridge over pain and time, and reach the cathartic recognition that will bracket out the horror of the death camps and open the way for a "normal" life; or will it, on the contrary, irreparably clinch his alienation not only from the world but from the supposed intimacy of his self-knowledge? Like Moshe then, the boy leaves it to a third party (a willing community or a mirror) to mediate between his present and past selves, and cancel out the alienating effect of his brush with inhumanity. Just like the town folks, however, the mirror does not cooperate. Instead of the familiar face that would have reconciled him with his former self (and consequently, with a pre-*Shoah* world), his reflection seals his alienation: "From the depth of the mirror, a corpse gazed back at me. The look in his eyes, as they stared into mine, has never left me."

Night is the story of a repeated dying, at once the death of man and of the *idea* of man. The final recognition never obtains. Instead, the subject is propelled out of himself, out of humanity, out of the world as he knew it. It is a double failure: both Moshe and the boy fail to recover their selves' integrity and to reintegrate into the community of the living; both fail to assimilate the traces left by their experience (either in a narrative or in a physiognomy) into a coherent picture to be accepted by the other(s) they so wish to reach. But the story goes on: *Night* is a first-person narrative. Like Moshe, the boy will try again to reintegrate the human community, this time, by telling his story (and many others). Like all survivors' narratives, *Night* is thus yet another plodding from door to door to solicit listeners, so as to reclaim one's ties to the community of the living by inscribing oneself into its shared narratives. . . .

Moshe and the town folks occupy two opposite ends of a transaction. Moshe wants the community to assimilate his story, to take it in and learn its lesson, in the hope that it will allow him a way out of the unbearable solitude into which his experience has cast him, and bridge over the tear that his encounter with the dispassionate force of evil has introduced in his life. . . . The town folk, however, do not want to take up this horror, to make it theirs, to make this story the *rallying point* between themselves and the narrator, since if they did, his burden would become theirs. . . .

DEALING WITH THE *SHOAH*

It has often been said that *Night* is the gloomy story of a loss for which no solace, no solution is offered. Indeed, "Elie Wiesel has repeatedly stated that survivors of the Holocaust live in a nightmare world that can never be understood. . . ." But it should also be noted that, although *Night* is the only novel in which he dealt directly and explicitly with his experience of the *Shoah*, Wiesel's whole life has been dedicated to its ensuing moral and historical imperatives. Moshe the Beadle (Wiesel's spokesman) thus offers a critique of facile answers to post-*Shoah* difficulties—narrowly individualized answers that, despite their limited usefulness, nonetheless overlook the collective dimension and its impact on the individual's self-positioning. Excessive separateness of past and present is yet another form of repression, another defense mechanism. The historical imperative today is not to "sort out" but, on the contrary, to find a way of *taking in* the reality of industrialized killing, knowing fully that this reality contradicts every aspect of our historical project, everything we would like to believe about ourselves. To date, we have not resolved this incongruity. If we are to deal with the legacy of the *Shoah*, we must make room in our project for the disturbing truths of the *Shoah*. Our historical imperative is to go beyond this contradiction and to integrate the lesson of the *Shoah* into the coherence of the stories and histories by which we define our sociohistorical project (by "project" I mean the future we wish upon ourselves as a society, and according to which we shape our present perception and representations of ourselves). None of us, therefore, escapes the need to "deal" with the *Shoah*; but none of us can do it alone.

Wiesel Talks About *Night* and Life After the Holocaust

Elie Wiesel, interviewed by Bob Costas

In a rare interview with Bob Costas—best known for being an award-winning sportscaster—Wiesel fills in some of the gaps in *Night* and talks about what his life was like after being liberated from the camp. The interview appeared on the NBC show *Later . . . with Bob Costas* in 1992, and it was only the second time in his life that Wiesel had talked about life in the concentration camps. Since *Night* can only scratch the surface of Wiesel's true experience, this interview gives the reader an invaluable piece of the puzzle.

BC: When they first gathered you up and took you from your home, were you actually hopeful? Could you rationalize some possibility, some outcome here, other than death, other than this unthinkable outcome?

EW: We didn't think of death. It happened in March—March 19, 1944, the Germans came into Hungary. Two months or so before the Normandy invasion. The Russians were very near. And then the ghetto arrived. Two weeks later, we were all in the ghetto. At night we would see the artillery exchange between the Russians and the Germans. They were only twenty kilometers away. We could have escaped. There was nothing to prevent us from escaping because there were two Germans, Eichmann and someone else, some fifty Hungarian gendarmes, and there was no problem. We could have left the ghetto into the mountains. We had non-Jewish friends who wanted us to come and stay with them. But we didn't know. We thought the war would end soon, and the Russians would come in, and Hitler would be defeated, and everything would come back to normalcy.

BC: When they loaded you all up and took you out of

Excerpted from "A Wound That Will Never Be Healed: An Interview with Elie Wiesel," by Bob Costas, in *Telling the Tale: A Tribute to Elie Wiesel on the Occasion of His 65th Birthday,* edited by Harry James Cargas. Copyright ©1993 by Time Being Press. Reprinted by permission of Time Being Books.

town, did you think then that this was the end of the line, or did you think that perhaps you would simply be detained for a while and, when the war ended, liberated?

EW: Well, the Germans had developed a psychology, a kind of mass psychology, how to fool, how to deceive the victims. And we were all victims. We didn't know. Until the very last moment, we believed that families would remain together, and we should be in some labor camp. Young people would work, and the parents would stay home and prepare food, meals. We didn't know until the very last minute, until it was too late.

THE DEHUMANIZING BEGINS

BC: I know that you'll never forget the words "Men to the left, women to the right." That's how they separated you from your mother and your sisters, you and your father.

EW: Well, of course, that was the real shock, the brutality of the words. The words were simple, "left" and "right," but what they meant, the meaning of those words, hit me much later. For three days or so I was in a haze. I thought I was dreaming. For three days I was dreaming. We were there in the shadow of the flames, and to me it wasn't real. I couldn't believe it. I write about it in *Night.* I couldn't believe it that in the twentieth century, in the middle of the twentieth century, people should do that, could do that, to other people. I somehow couldn't accept it, and to this day I cannot accept it. Something in me rejects that notion that would dehumanize a killer to such an extent. And the complicity, the indifference of the world—this, to this day, it moves me to anger.

BC: When they tattooed a number on your arm, was that the single most dehumanizing moment, or is it just one, in a litany of dehumanizing moments?

EW: Oh, that didn't mean a thing, but the first dehumanizing incident was the day when we arrived, really. (I mean the next day—we arrived at night.) And there was a Kapo, and my father went to him saying he would like to go to the toilet. And my father was a respectful man. And the Kapo hit him in his face, and my father fell to the ground. That was the beginning of the experience really, that I, his only son, couldn't come to his help. Usually I should have thrown myself at the tormentor and beat him up. But that was the first realization there that he and I were already in prison, and not only I, but my mind is in prison, my soul is in prison, my being is in prison, and I am no longer free to do what I want to do. . . .

BC: What were the most conspicuous examples of heroism, under the circumstances, that you saw, and were there examples of cowardice that you saw among the captive Jews?

EW: Cowardice is a word that we didn't apply because, logically, everyone should have been a coward—could have been and probably was because one SS man with a machine gun was stronger than a thousand poets. Heroism . . . I've seen heroism, a spectacular kind of heroism, which I described when three members of the underground were hanged, and the way they faced the execution was heroic. But then I've seen heroism in a simple way. Let's say a man who would come to us on the Sabbath—I don't even know his name—and would simply say, "Don't forget that today is *Shabbat.*" Don't forget that today is Sabbath. To us it meant nothing, because how could it? Same thing, Sabbath, Sunday, Monday. We were all destined to be killed. The fact that he said, "Don't forget that it is the Sabbath, a sacred day." Or somebody would come and say, "Don't forget your name. You are not only a number, you have a name." I've seen people giving their bread to their comrades whom they didn't know. I've seen a person who has offered himself to be beaten up instead of somebody else, whom he didn't know. In general, you know, the enemy, the killers, what they wanted to do there was to dehumanize the victim by depriving him of all moral values. Therefore the first lesson that they gave us was you are alone; don't count on anyone, don't think of anyone, only of yourself. You are alone, and only you should matter to yourself. And they were wrong. Because those who did care for somebody else—a father for his father, a son for his father, a friend for a friend—I think they lived longer because they felt committed, which means humanity became heroic in their own hearts.

A Son's Guilt

BC: As I said, you and your father were separated, as they broke the men and the women apart, from your mother and your sisters, and you would never see your younger sister or your mother again; they perished. The theme of *Night* (your first book) that runs through the whole thing is your father trying to support you, you trying to support your father, at all costs not becoming separated from each other. And then just one of the tragic facts of those years is that your father finally succumbed only months before the U.S. forces liberated the concentration camp.

EW: As long as my father was alive, I was alive. When he died, I was no longer alive. It wasn't life; it was something else. I existed, but I didn't live. And even when we were together we had a certain code. We didn't talk about my mother, my sisters. We didn't talk. We were afraid. There were certain things in those times and in those places that people cannot understand today. We didn't cry. People didn't cry inside that universe. Maybe because people were afraid if they were to start crying, they would never end. But people didn't cry. Even when there were selections and somebody left somebody else, there were no tears. It was something so harsh—the despair was so harsh—that it didn't dissolve itself in tears, or in prayers either.

BC: You saw the reverse, though, too. I mean, you detail situations where a son beat his father because that was the way he thought, at least temporarily, to get into the good graces of his captors; a situation where a younger, stronger son took a morsel of bread from his dying father.

EW: Yes, I've seen, but there were very few, really, in truth, there were few. It's normal. But what happened there, the killers managed to create a universe parallel to our own. The kind of creation, a parallel creation, and there they established their own society with its own rulers, with its own philosophers, its own psychologists, its own poets, with a new society outside God, outside humanity. And, naturally, some succumbed. I cannot even judge them. I cannot be angry at them. Imagine a child of twelve arriving in Auschwitz, and he knows that only violence could be a refuge. Either he becomes an author of violence or a victim of violence. So, a child of twelve overnight aged and became an old person. How can I judge such a child? He didn't do it. He was made to do it by—he was conditioned to do it—by the tormentor. If I am angry, I am angry at the tormentor, not at the victim.

BC: Toward the end of *Night,* you describe your father's death. And he did not go to the furnaces, except to burn his corpse. He died of dysentery and a combination of the hardships.

EW: The hunger. Hunger and exhaustion, fatigue.

BC: And the last night, he was calling out to you for water, but at the same time a guard was beating him. And your best judgment was that you couldn't help him. You were helpless; you didn't respond. And then you write, "There were no prayers at his grave. No candles were lit to his memory. His last word was my name. A summons to which I did not respond." You couldn't possibly feel guilt about that, if you are being hard on yourself.

EW: I do, I do. I do feel guilt. I know that logically I shouldn't, but I do feel guilty because we were terribly close. We became very close there. But, at the same time, the instinct prevented me from being killed. If I had moved, I would have been killed. Beaten up to death. I was as weak as he was. And who would have known that he would die that night? And we didn't know. But I do feel guilty.

BEARING WITNESS

BC: You saw a child, who you described as having the face of an angel—saw that child hanged. That's one of the most moving passages in the book. This is (obviously you have steeled yourself) your life's work, to tell of these things, so that's why I feel no reluctance to ask you to tell again, but how does somebody watch these things—these things unthinkable if we read them in fiction—unfold and then find some reason to keep on living?

EW: Well, first, you know, I don't speak about this often. I have written a few books, very few. I prefer, I think, books on the Talmud and the Bible. And through them, I transmit certain obsessions, certain fears, or certain memories. At that time it was my father who kept me alive. We saw it together. And I wanted him to live. I knew that if I die, he will die. And that was the reason I could eat after having seen that scene, the hanging, And I remember it well, I remember it now. I didn't forget a single instant, a single episode.

BC: Did you assume, as you and your father tried as best you could to survive, that your mother and your sister were dead?

EW: Oh, we knew, but we didn't talk about it. I knew. He knew. At one point only, the very first night, when we were walking toward the flames—we didn't know yet anything, but we were walking toward the flames—my father said, "Maybe you should have gone with your mother." Had I gone with my mother, I would have been killed that night too. But we never talked about this. There was a kind of rule: we

don't talk about it, about those who are absent, bec
hurts too much. We couldn't accept such pain.

BC: Everyone, except those deranged and hateful sou
who try to propound this preposterous theory that the Holocaust didn't occur, knows it occurred, and, statistically, they
understand the dimensions of it. But until one hears the stories of Holocaust survivors and just a tiny number of the
hundreds of thousands of particulars, until you hear that,
you can't begin to grasp the ghastly horror of it. There is just
no way, if you stood on a mountaintop for five thousand
years and screamed to the top of your lungs, to overstate it.

EW: We cannot *overstate* it. We must *understate* it. To
make it understandable, we must understate it. That's why
in this little book, *Night*, which has few pages actually, what
I *don't* say is important, as important as the things that I *do*
say. But even if you read all the books, all the documents, by
all the survivors, you would still not know. Unfortunately,
only those who were there know what it meant being there.
And yet we try. One of my first goals, really, was to write for
the survivors. I wanted them to write. In the beginning we
didn't speak. Nobody spoke. We felt, who would understand?
Who would believe? And why talk? And, really, the main
reason for writing *Night* was not for the world or for history;
it was for them. Look, it's important to bear witness. Important to tell your story. At the same time I know that even if all
the stories were to be read by one person—the same person—you would still not know. You cannot imagine what it
meant spending a night of death among death. . . .

How Could They Do It?

BC: Did you ever see any humanity in the actions or in the
eyes of your captors, any humanity at all?

EW: I did not.

BC: How do you suppose it is possible to purge humanity
from so many people?

EW: Bob, this is the question of my life. After the war, I
had a series of shocks, and one of the shocks was when I discovered that the commanders of the so-called *Einsatzkom-
mando,* that did firing in Eastern Europe, meaning in the
Ukraine and Russia, had college degrees. Some of them had
Ph.D.s, and that, to me, an educator—I am a professor, I
teach, I write—I can't understand it. What happened? Culture is supposed to be a shield, a moral shield. What hap-

' I don't understand that to this day. . . .

:e to face with Dr. Joseph Mengele, who

rried a baton in his hand, an almost the-

icter. Can you describe him beyond that?

ing opera while he was doing what he

id sing melodies from opera. I heard it

om people who worked with him, inmates.
He was an intelligent man, intellectual, polite. He even developed friendships with Jews, or with Gypsy children. There was a Gypsy camp, and he got fond of one of the Gypsy children, and his fondness then was translated in his own personal care of him: he took him to the gas chamber. The young Gypsy child whom he loved and caressed and embraced and kissed. I don't understand what happened to humanity, in the human being. I don't know. . . .

BC: A question which every kid with a high school education has heard, even one who's given scant thought to philosophy, is, if there is a God, how does God allow something like a Holocaust to happen?

EW: I don't know. If there is an answer, it is the wrong answer. But you see it's wrong, I think, to put everything on God's shoulders. That is something I understood later. Where was man? Where was humanity? Look, after all, we had faith in humanity—I had faith in humanity. To us, President Roosevelt was more important than Ben-Gurion. I had never heard of the name of Ben-Gurion in my little town. But I knew the name of Roosevelt. I remember we said prayers for him. He was the father of the Jewish people. He knew. Absolutely he knew. And yet he refused to bomb the railways going to Auschwitz. Why? Had he done that—at that time, during the Hungarian deportation, ten thousand Jews were killed every day in Auschwitz. Even if the Germans had tried to repair the rail . . .

BC: So even as the U.S. waged war against the Axis powers, you're saying they didn't do enough to hit the specific targets. They could have stopped that cold.

EW: They could have. Look . . . they . . . I admire the American soldiers who fought Hitler, and I think we should be eternally grateful to them, to their families, to their children, to their parents. Many died in the war. They were heroes. But somehow the war that Hitler had waged against the Jewish people was forgotten. In the process. And that was wrong. A few bombing operations would have at least shown Hitler that the world cared. Hitler was convinced to the end that the world didn't care about what he and his acolytes had done to the Jewish people. . . .

GETTING OUT

BC: Do you recall what you saw and what you felt the day the troops liberated Buchenwald in April of 1945?

EW: It was April 11, 1945, in the morning hours. We were the last remnants in Buchenwald, and I had been already at the gate almost every day. And, by accident, really, by chance, that the gate closed in front of me. So I came back to the camp. I remember when they came in. We were then already terribly hungry, more than usual because no food was given to us for six days, since April 5th. And I remember the first American soldiers. I remember black soldiers. I remember a black sergeant, huge. And then he saw us; he began sobbing and cursing. He was so moved by what he saw that he began sobbing—he sobbed like a child, and we couldn't console him. And we tried somehow to console him, and that made him sob even deeper, stronger, louder. So I remember those soldiers, and I have a weak—a soft spot—for the American soldier, really. I gave a lecture a few years ago at West Point, and it was amusing to me. I never had any military training or military affinity, and I came to give a lecture, and I told them what I felt about the American uniform, because that meant not only victory, it meant a triumph, the triumph of humanity. And to me, that black sergeant incarnates that triumph.

BC: Toward the end of *Night,* you write about looking into a mirror. Apparently, you didn't have any access to a mirror for two years. What did you see when you looked into that mirror?

EW: Well, when the Americans came in they threw us food, and it was the wrong thing to do because they should have used medical supervision, and they didn't. And I remember I picked up a can, some dessert, something with ham in it. Now during the camp, I would have eaten anything, but I was already free, and my body knew it even before I did, and I put it to my lips and passed out, literally; I got some blood poisoning. So, I woke up in a hospital, a former SS hospital which was taken over by the Americans for inmates. So, I almost died. I was, I think, closer to death after the liberation than before. And then one day, really, I saw myself in that

mirror. And I saw a person who was ageless, nameless, face-
less. A person who belonged to another world, the world of
the dead.

BC: If you belonged to the world of the dead (especially after your father slipped away from you only several weeks before the liberation came, which—the sad irony—just adds to
the heartache), if you were dead inside at that point, from
where did you summon the strength to direct a life so pur-
poseful in the ensuing forty-plus years?

EW: In the beginning it was again, I repeat, a passion for
study. I studied. I came to France together with four hundred
youngsters, children, orphans, invited by DeGaulle. And we
were taken over by an organization in a children's home, an
orphans' home. And the first thing I did, when I came there,
I asked for pen and paper. I began writing my memoirs. And
for quotations of the Talmud to study. It's later that I developed that since I am alive, I have to give meaning to my life.
Oh, it may sound, you know, bombastic, but it is true. That
is how I switched. That means that my life as it is, if it is only
for myself, then it is wrong. I have to do something with it. I
even have to do something with my memory of my death. . . .

THE AFTERLIFE

BC: Did you ever, subsequent to Auschwitz, come face to
face with Gestapo officers?

EW: No.

BC: Former Nazis? Not once?

EW: No. I came face to face, and I wrote about it in one of
my books, in Israel, during the Eichmann trial. I saw Eichmann at the trial, but he was in a glass cage. But later, I saw,
in a bus, going from Tel Aviv to Jerusalem, a man that I—I
recognized his neck. He was a kind of blockhouse, or barracks, head in Auschwitz. My barracks head. And I passed
him, and all of a sudden I said, "Tell me, where were you during the war?" And he said, "Why?" And I said, "Aren't you a
German Jew? Weren't you in Poland?" He said, "Yes."
"Weren't you in Auschwitz?" "Yes." "In the barracks?" "Yes." I
gave him the number, at which point he paled because had I
said, "You were a head of a barracks," they would have beaten
him up during the Eichmann trial, and for a few seconds, I
became his judge. Literally, I had his fate in my hands. And
then, I decided, I am not a judge; I am a witness. I let him go.

BC: You understand, of course, the passion that fuels the

work of so-called Nazi hunters. But your position has been different. Yours is to bear witness . . .

EW: Yes.

BC: . . . rather than to exact revenge or even pursue justice.

EW: Well, pursue justice, yes. But it's not my doing; I cannot do that. I admire those people who are doing it very well, and there are several of these young people, young people who dedicate their lives for the pursuit of justice, and all honor is due them. But my work is something else. I write. I teach. And I bear witness in my way. That doesn't mean I'm better, not at all, or worse. I don't think so. Except we all have our area of competence and activity. . . .

BC: Please, don't think for a moment that this question is intended to trivialize the most important aspects of your experience, but I think people who admire you would wonder about it. Are there moments of gaiety and spontaneous laughter in your life, or is the enormity of this experience such that it is always with you, that there is a certain solemnity about you at all times?

EW: Oh, no, no. Really not. I laugh, and I am happy, and I love good concerts, and I love my good friends, and we tell jokes to each other. And then I give lectures at the Y, for instance, or at Boston University. I try to introduce as much humor . . . no, I am not a person who believes in macabre or serious despairing moods. Nonsense. I don't have the right to impose that upon anybody else, the opposite: I like good cheer and good theatre and good comedies, and, in general, I think life is not only tears. Life also has happiness to offer and to receive.

BC: Do you worry that as Jewish culture becomes less distinct, at least here in America, and there are pockets of exceptions to that in the Hasidic community, or whatever, but as Jewish culture becomes less distinct and as generational memory blurs as we move further and further from the Holocaust, that the meaning of this will slip further into the ash heap of history, and as witnesses grow older and perish . . .

EW: I do worry. I am not afraid that the event will be forgotten. There were many years in my life that I was afraid that it will be, might be, forgotten. And, therefore, I try to work. I try to inspire and to convince many of my friends also to work. Now I know it won't be forgotten because there are enough documents and books and pictures and even masterworks that will prevent people from forgetting. Today, if I am afraid, and I am afraid, it is that the event will be trivialized, cheapened, reduced to commercial kitsch. That is a source of anguish.

You Have to Be Taught to Hate

BC: At least once in this conversation, but I think only once, you used the word "hatred." No one could blame anybody who was even witness to this, let alone victim of it (and you were both) for hating everybody involved. But hate can consume a person as they move through their life. How have you subdued it or channeled it?

EW: At times I missed it, I wanted it. There were times when I even wrote; I said, we need some kind of hatred. It's normal, it's natural, to channel this hate out, to drive it out, but to *experience* it. Why I didn't—during the war I had other problems on my mind. My father. You know, I really didn't *see* the Germans. I saw the Germans as angels of death. I couldn't lift my eyes. It was forbidden to lift my eyes to see a German SS because he would kill you. After the war, I had my problems: how to readjust, how to readjust to death. It was more difficult to readjust to death than to life, to see in death an exception to the rule, not the normative phenomenon. It was difficult because we were used to death as a normative experience. We lived in death; we lived with death. And then to think about death as a scandal, as a tragedy—it took me some time. So we had to do so many things, really, after the war, to find myself again, and to find the language, to find a life, to find a destiny, to find a family, that I didn't think about that, about hatred. But I knew that it had to exist because it was on the other side. And that's why, since the Nobel Prize, really, I've devoted years to organize seminars all over the world called "Anatomy of Hate." I want to understand the power, the destructive power, of hate. The masks that hate can put on. The language of hate, the technique of hate, the structure of hate, the fabric of hate, the genesis of hate.

BC: Is there a single insight about that that you've come to, that you feel certain of?

EW: I learned from those who participated in a few of my seminars—psychiatrists—saying that a child, until the age of three, doesn't hate. Children can be taught to hate after they are three years old. That means something.

A Letter to Wiesel Questions *Night*'s Preface

Eva Fleischner

In the form of a letter directed to Elie Wiesel, Eva
Fleischner, professor of religion and philosophy at
Montclair State College in New Jersey, wonders
whether it is still necessary and valid to include
François Mauriac's preface to *Night* (from the original
publication in 1958) in new editions of the book today.
When the preface was originally written it may have
needed the introduction from this famous Catholic
writer, but now it can certainly stand on its own.

Dear Elie:

Whenever I use *Night* in my classes, I tell my students:
"Be sure to read Mauriac's Preface. Not all prefaces deserve
to be read, but this one does. It will give you a key to the
book." All these years *Night* has remained linked to Mauriac's name. This had always seemed quite normal to me,
even fitting. After all, it was Mauriac who, in your own
words, had launched you as a writer. I can imagine that it
had been an honor for you—at the time a young, unknown
Jewish journalist—to have the famous French writer and
member of the *Académie Française* introduce your first
book, and thus introduce you to the world.

But decades have gone by. You no longer need Mauriac to
introduce you to the world. The world knows you well. You
have written many other books, each new book eagerly
awaited. You have received the Nobel Peace Prize. Mauriac is
dead. And yet, you have kept his Preface as prelude to *Night*,
and thereby as prelude to your entire work. What may have
been grateful acceptance on your part decades ago has long
since become deliberate choice.

Could this choice have had its moments of difficulty for

Excerpted from "Mauriac's Preface to *Night:* Thirty Years Later," by Eva Fleischner,
America, November 19, 1988. Reprinted with permission from the author.

you? I wonder about this because of all that Mauriac represents, not only in literature (fame and success), but also in
religion (Catholicism). Given the profoundly tragic history
of the relationship between your faith and his (and mine),
was it really so easy for you to accept the endorsement of
your work by France's leading Catholic writer? All the more
so because, as you make vividly clear in "An Interview Unlike Any Other," Mauriac's approach to Judaism was cast—
at least initially, and quite understandably—in the mold
common, prior to Vatican II, even to those Catholics who
were sympathetic to Judaism. At best—as you mentioned in
A Jew Today—they saw Judaism as no more than a prelude
to Christianity, as the setting for Jesus: "Every reference led
back to him. Jerusalem? The eternal city, where Jesus
turned his disciples into apostles. The Bible? The Old Testament, which, thanks to Jesus of Nazareth, succeeded in en-
riching itself with a New Testament. Mendes-France? A Jew,
both brave and hated, not unlike Jesus long ago." You leave
no doubt in the reader's mind how deeply these words offended the Jew in you—to the point where, for the first time
in your life, you "exhibited bad manners." So great was your
anger that it overcame your shyness and you wounded the
old man with your words, and he began to weep.

You allowed yourself to be angry, and he allowed himself
to weep. Each of you had the courage to be in touch with
who you truly were at that moment. And it was this that
broke down the wall between you. There is no downplaying
of the moment of harshness. Mauriac's humanity made him
weep over his insensitivity to you as Jew. Your humanity
caused you to be deeply troubled because you had hurt an
upright and profoundly moral man.

Your humanity, Elie, has seemed to me to be the constant
in your life. No matter how much has changed for you and
in you these long years, you are no longer homeless and
alone. You have a beloved wife and son; you are revered the
world over. This has not changed. If, at times, your judgment
of Christianity has seemed harsh to me, in your personal in-
teractions, whether with me or with my students or with the
many Christian friends who love you, there has never been
anything but gentleness and graciousness.

And is it any wonder that you should judge Christianity
harshly? That, even as a child, you would cross the street out
of fear whenever you passed a church? No, it is no wonder;

it is, alas, all too understandable. For Christians have incurred much guilt toward your people. What is surprising, what is extraordinary, is that you have been able to distinguish between the tradition as a whole, and individual Christians. For this I have long been grateful to you.

Recently, since reading your new book *Twilight,* I am grateful in yet another way. For I sense in this book a change in your attitude. Not only is the hero, Raphael, saved by two

---

A CHRISTIAN WEEPS

When François Mauriac, one of France's best known Christian writers, met Wiesel in the 1950s, he encouraged him to tell his story. In Mauriac's Foreword (preface) to the resulting book, Night, *he explains how Wiesel's story allowed him to recognize the extent of the Jews' suffering at the hands of the Germans.*

The child who tells us his story here was one of God's elect. From the time when his conscience first awoke, he had lived only for God and had been reared on the Talmud, aspiring to initiation into the cabbala, dedicated to the Eternal. Have we ever thought about the consequence of a horror that, though less apparent, less striking than the other outrages, is yet the worst of all to those of us who have faith: the death of God in the soul of a child who suddenly discovers absolute evil? . . .

And I, who believe that God is love, what answer could I give my young questioner, whose dark eyes still held the reflection of that angelic sadness which had appeared one day upon the face of the hanged child? What did I say to him? Did I speak of that other Jew, his brother, who may have resembled him—the Crucified, whose Cross has conquered the world? Did I affirm that the stumbling block to his faith was the cornerstone of mine, and that the conformity between the Cross and the suffering of men was in my eyes the key to that impenetrable mystery whereon the faith of his childhood had perished? Zion, however, has risen up again from the crematories and the charnel houses. The Jewish nation has been resurrected from among its thousands [now known to be six million] of dead. It is through them that it lives again. We do not know the worth of one single drop of blood, one single tear. All is grace. If the Eternal is the Eternal, the last word for each one of us belongs to Him. This is what I should have told this Jewish child. But I could only embrace him, weeping.

François Mauriac, *Forward to* Night, New York: Hill and Wang, 1960, pp. viii–xi.

peasants "who are good Christians," but in describing the age-old pogroms that used to break out during Holy Week in Rovidok (as in so many other villages and towns of eastern Europe) you speak of the perpetrators as "Christians who were not necessarily followers of Christ."

Why do these few words move me so? Let me try to explain. For us Christians, the sense of guilt at our corporate history of persecution of Jews becomes, at times, almost too heavy to bear. The burden is lightened when we discover, or remember, that there have been through the centuries Christian women and men who did not run with the mob, even—also—during that darkest of times that will forever be known as the Holocaust.

Because of the weight your words carry for millions of people, non-Jews as well as Jews, the text I have quoted can, and I believe will, make a crucial contribution to the reconciliation between our two peoples. Thus, more than ever will you have become the messenger of peace the Nobel Peace Prize citation calls you.

And perhaps, also, your relationship with your old friend François Mauriac will have entered a new phase. Were you to talk once more face to face today yet another barrier between you would have fallen. Perhaps, indeed, the dialogue continues? After all, both Jews and Christians worship a "God who raises the dead."

Permit me to end these reflections with a wish. Won't you, please, as you promised in *A Jew Today*, publish your conversations with Mauriac, which continued over the years? Then we would know a little more of the relationship between you, of what enabled you both to transcend your religious and political disagreements. Only you can give us answers to this and, by so doing, shed further light on one of the most remarkable friendships of this century.

Happy birthday, and Shalom!

CHRONOLOGY

1928

Elie Wiesel is born on September 30, in Sighet, Transylvania (originally part of Romania, at the time of the World War II it was part of Hungary) to Shlomo and Sarah. Two daughters, Hilda and Bea precede him, and another, Tzipora, is born a few years later.

1930

The Nazi Party gains a stronghold in the German government.

1933

Adolf Hitler is elected chancellor of Germany and begins his war against the Jews. The SS and Gestapo are created. The first Nazi death camp is built in Dachau, Germany. All Jewish teachers and government workers are fired.

1934

Hitler becomes führer.

1934–1944

Wiesel studies the Torah, Talmud, and cabbala and enjoys a happy childhood in his tightly-knit Jewish community.

1935

The Nuremberg Laws limiting the freedom of Jews are decreed.

1937

Another concentration camp, Buchenwald, opens in Germany and begins exterminating Jews.

1938

Delegates from thirty-two countries meet in France to discuss saving the Jews from Hitler; no one offers to accept them. German Jews are forced into ghettos. In one night, called Kristallnacht (the Night of Broken Glass), nearly 7,500 Jewish-owned businesses and 267 synagogues are destroyed.

1940

Auschwitz is built near Warsaw in Poland and becomes the Nazi's largest concentration camp.

1944

The Nazis deport Wiesel's family to Auschwitz, where his mother and younger sister are killed. Wiesel is imprisoned in Auschwitz and Buna.

1945

Wiesel and his father join the death march to Buchenwald, where his father dies. Wiesel is freed by Russian soldiers on April 10. World War II ends in Europe in May and Wiesel goes to France.

1946

Wiesel studies French in Paris and is reunited with his two older sisters, who had presumed him dead. He teaches Bible, Yiddish, and Hebrew. The Nuremberg trials begin.

1947–1950

Wiesel studies philosophy, literature, and psychology at the Sorbonne, University of Paris.

1948

Israel becomes an independent Jewish state. Wiesel becomes a foreign correspondent for various Jewish news organizations.

1952

Anne Frank's *Diary of a Young Girl* is published in English.

1954

Wiesel interviews famous French writer François Mauriac who convinces him to tell the story of his experiences at the hands of the Nazis.

1956

Wiesel publishes an 862-page memoir, written in Yiddish, titled *Un di Velt Hot Geshvign* (*And the World Remained Silent*). During a trip to New York City to report on the United Nations he is struck by a taxi. While recovering, he applies for U.S. citizenship.

1958

A much shortened version of his Yiddish memoir is published in France under the title *La Nuit.*

1960

The English version of *La Nuit*, called *Night*, is published in America.

1961

Wiesel's first novel, *Dawn*, is published in America.

1962

The Accident is published.

1963

Wiesel receives U.S. citizenship.

1964

Wiesel visits Sighet, his hometown. *The Town Beyond the Wall* is published.

1966

Jews of Silence and *The Gates of the Forest* are published.

1968

A Beggar in Jerusalem is published in France, and wins the Prix Medicis, one of France's most distinguished literary awards.

1969

Wiesel marries Marion Rose, who becomes the translator of most of his books.

1970

One Generation After is published, marking twenty-five years since Wiesel was freed from Buchenwald.

1972

Wiesel's son, Shlomo Elisha, is born. Wiesel receives the Eleanor Roosevelt Memorial Award and the American Liberties Medallion, and is appointed distinguished professor of Jewish studies at the City College of New York. *Souls on Fire* is published.

1973

The Oath is published. Wiesel is awarded the Martin Luther King Medallion from the City College of New York and the Jewish Book Council Literary Award.

1974

Wiesel's play, *The Madness of God*, is performed in Washington, D.C.

1976

Wiesel is appointed Andrew Mellon Professor in the Humanities at Boston University. *Messengers of God* is published.

1979

President Jimmy Carter appoints Wiesel Chairman of the Presidential Commission on the Holocaust, later re-named the U.S. Holocaust Memorial Council.

1980

Wiesel is appointed Honorary Chairman of the World Gathering of Jewish Holocaust Survivors, Jerusalem. *The Testament* is published.

1983

Wiesel is awarded the Belgian International Peace Prize.

1985

Wiesel is awarded the Congressional Gold Medal of Achievement by President Ronald Reagan. *The Fifth Son* is published and wins the Grand Prize for literature from the city of Paris.

1986

Wiesel is awarded the Nobel Peace Prize for "his self-accepted mission as a messenger to mankind: his message is one of peace, atonement and human dignity." He establishes the Elie Wiesel Foundation for Humanity to "create forums for the discussion of urgent ethical and moral issues confronting mankind."

1992

President George Bush awards Wiesel the Presidential Medal of Freedom. *The Forgotten* is published.

1993

Wiesel speaks at the dedication of the U.S. Holocaust Memorial Museum in Washington, D.C.

1995

Wiesel publishes the first volume of his memoirs, *All Rivers Run to the Sea.*

2000

Wiesel publishes the second volume of his memoirs, *And the Sea Is Never Full.* By this time he has been awarded nearly eighty honorary degrees from some of the world's most prestigious universities.

For Further Research

Works by Elie Wiesel

The Accident. Trans. Anne Borchardt. New York: Avon, 1962.

All Rivers Run to the Sea: Memoirs. New York: Knopf, 1995.

Ani Maamin. Trans. Marion Wiesel. New York: Random House, 1973.

A Beggar in Jerusalem. Trans. Lily Edelman and Elie Wiesel. New York: Random House, 1970.

Dawn. Trans. Frances Frenaye. New York: Hill & Wang, 1961.

Dimensions of the Holocaust. Evanston, IL: Northwestern University Press, 1977.

Evil and Exile. Trans. Jan Rothschild. Notre Dame, IN: University of Notre Dame Press, 1990.

The Fifth Son. Trans. Marion Wiesel. New York: Summit Books, 1985.

Five Biblical Portraits. Notre Dame, IN: University of Notre Dame Press, 1978.

The Forgotten. New York: Summit Books, 1992.

Four Hasidic Masters and Their Stuggle Against Melancholy. Notre Dame, IN: University of Notre Dame Press, 1978.

From the Kingdom of Memory: Reminiscences. New York: Summit Books, 1990.

The Gates of the Forest. Trans. Frances Frenaye. New York: Holt, Rinehart and Winston, 1966.

The Golem. New York: Summit Books, 1983.

The Jews of Silence. Trans. Neal Kozodoy. New York: Holt, Rinehart and Winston, 1966.

A Jew Today. Trans. Marion Wiesel. New York: Random House, 1978.

A Journey into Faith. New York: Donald I. Fine, 1990.

Legends of Our Time. New York: Avon, 1968.

Messengers of God. Trans. Marion Wiesel. New York: Random House, 1976.

Night. Trans. Stella Rodway. New York: Hill & Wang, 1960.

The Oath. New York: Avon, 1973.

One Generation After. New York: Pocket Books, 1970.

Sages and Dreamers. New York: Summit Books, 1991.

Somewhere a Master. Trans. Marion Wiesel. New York: Summit Books, 1982.

Souls on Fire. Trans. Marion Wiesel. New York: Random House, 1972.

The Testament. Trans. Marion Wiesel. New York: Summit Books, 1981.

The Town Beyond the Wall. Trans. Stephen Becker. New York: Avon, 1964.

The Trial of God. Trans. Marion Wiesel. New York: Random House, 1979. (Play)

Twilight. Trans. Marion Wiesel. New York: Summit Books, 1988.

ANALYSIS AND CRITICISM

Irving Abrahamson, ed., *Against Silence: The Voice and Vision of Elie Wiesel.* 3 vols. New York: Holocaust Library, 1985.

Michael Berenbaum, *The Vision of the Void: Theological Reflections on the Works of Elie Wiesel.* Middletown, CT: Wesleyan University Press, 1979.

Harry James Cargas, *Harry James Cargas in Conversation with Elie Wiesel.* New York: Paulist Press, 1976.

Ellen S. Fine, *Legacy of Night.* Albany: State University of New York Press, 1982.

Irving Greenberg and Alvin Rosenfeld, eds., *Confronting the Holocaust: The Impact of Elie Wiesel.* Bloomington: Indiana University Press, 1978.

Irving Halperin, *Messengers from the Dead: Literature of the Holocaust.* Philadelphia: Westminster Press, 1970.

Carol Rittner, ed., *Elie Wiesel: Between Memory and Hope.* New York: New York University Press, 1990.

Simon P. Sibelman, *Silence in the Novels of Elie Wiesel.* New York: St. Martin's Press, 1995.

BIOGRAPHIES

Ted L. Estess, *Elie Wiesel.* New York: Frederick Ungar, 1980.

Michael A. Schuman, *Elie Wiesel: Voice from the Holocaust.* Berkeley Heights, NJ: Enslow Publishers, 1994.

HISTORICAL INTEREST

David A. Adler, *We Do Remember the Holocaust.* New York: Henry Holt, 1989.

Anne Frank, *The Diary of a Young Girl.* New York: Doubleday, 1952.

Daniel Jonah Goldhagen, *Hitler's Willing Executioners: Ordinary Germans and the Holocaust.* New York:Knopf, 1996.

Lawrence D. Kritzman, ed., *Auschwitz and After.* New York: Routledge, 1995.

Primo Levi, *Survival in Auschwitz.* New York: Collier, 1959.

Lois Lowry, *Number the Stars.* Boston: Houghton Mifflin, 1989.

Han Nolan, *If I Should Die Before I Wake.* San Diego: Harcourt Brace, 1994.

Hana Volavkova, ed., *I Never Saw Another Butterfly.* New York: Schocken, 1978.

David W. Zisenwine, *Anti-Semitism in Europe: Sources of the Holocaust.* New York: Behrman House, 1976.

INDEX